the Adversary

the Adversary

THE CHRISTIAN VERSUS DEMON ACTIVITY

MARK I. BUBECK

MOODY PRESS

CHICAGO

Moody Press, a ministry of the Moody Bible Institute, is
designed for education, evangelization and edification.
If we may assist you in knowing more about Christ and
the Christian life, please write us without obligation to:
Moody Press, c/o MLM, Chicago, Illinois 60610.

30

Printed in the United States of America

To
My Victory Partners

My wife, Anita; my daughters,
Judy, Donna, and Rhonda and her
husband, Gary.

ACKNOWLEDGMENTS

Special appreciation is due numerous friends who granted permission to use illustrations out of their personal lives. Thanks also to Mrs. Rose Kammerling, who typed the manuscript as an act of friendship and as a labor of love to her Lord.

CONTENTS

FOREWORD

When Mark Bubeck and I were undergraduates at the Moody Bible Institute twenty-five years ago, it seemed that nearly no one in the sophisticated Western world, except the inner Catholic and fundamentalist circles, believed in the devil. Science was in vogue, while seances were relegated to eccentric wierdos who were too neurotic to come to grips with reality. To subscribe to a belief in Satan was tantamount to believing in Halloween goblins, the bogeyman, or guardian angels. Secularists reckoned that once society could afford enough psychiatrists to eliminate depressions on one hand, or irrational hallucinations on the other, it would be rid of the ills which imbalanced the march of man toward his self-proclaimed utopia.

. Man must worship. Turning his back on God, he still found himself with what some have called "the God-shaped blank" within. And the devil, whom he had pushed out through the window of his mind, would then come crashing back in through the door of his heart. Today he is ubiquitous. What we used to think was the special monopoly of primitive peoples—like the pagan barbarians of the Congo or the heathen-hearted savages of Borneo jungles—has moved into fashionable suburbia. Voodoo, fortune telling, black magic, witchcraft, poltergeistism, spiritism with mediums, parapsychology clinics (which often are no more nor less than seances with professors as the mediums)—they're everywhere. It's not legal to have Christianity in sharp focus in academe, but the devil—the red carpet has been rolled out to him! Demonizing denizens seem to be in the highest style today.

A few years ago Mick Jagger and his Rolling Stones came out with the song, "Sympathy for the Devil," and it spread like the Spanish influenza, climaxing in a film, *The Blood, Sweat and Tears*. Their *Symphony to the Devil* moved from service to Satan to the worship of Satan. The last estimate I heard was that one in four current pop songs has, woven into its lyrics somewhere, a salute to Satan.

Then came a tremendous rush of films which featured the devil, such as *The Devil in Miss Jones* and *Rosemary's Baby*. Is it any wonder that huge and violent gangs of youth are bamboozled by this kind of propaganda into calling themselves Satan's Choice, Hell's Angels, Hell's Belles, and The Devil's Disciples?

Then there are the books—both serious and bizarre—featuring the devil in their titles and enticing people to read. The phenomenon carries into the horoscopes and astrology charts which are published in fifteen hundred of North America's two thousand daily newspapers and followed with far more devotion than most Christians follow the Word of God.

There are television programs on Satanism every week. Pick up a TV guide and run down through program titles, and you will be astonished at how many there are. And there are the magazine articles—three cover stories in nine months in *Time*, for example.

Nor is it something exclusive to Western society. It is perhaps even stronger in the communist world; *The Los Angeles Times* tells us that whole villages are under the domination of witches and wizards. And of course it is strongest in the third world where the name of Christ has been least known.

I firmly believe in the work which Mark Bubeck has done herein, based on his intimate knowledge of Christ, of the Bible, and of people.

Mark and I met at Moody. Fifteen years later we were together at his invitation for several months in Denver, where he was pastor of a great church; and where I saw as saintly a man of God as I have ever known. His treatment of the devil in this book is thorough, biblical, balanced, and gives answers to questions which are being asked today, not just by the tiny minority of Bible-believing Christians, but by the vast majority of people everywhere, who in the present explosion of Satan worship and demonism, are wondering what truly is the Word of God. The scripture passage which struck me again and again as I read through this book was the apostle Paul's description: "The Lord's bond-servant must not be quarrelsome, but be kind to all, able to teach, patient when wronged, with gentleness correcting those who are in opposition, if perhaps God may grant them repentance leading to the knowledge of the truth, and they may come to their senses and escape the snare of the devil, having been held captive by him to do his will" (2 Timothy 2:24-26, NASB). Mark Bubeck is such a servant.

JOHN WESLEY WHITE

PREFACE

"Consider mine enemies, for they are many; and they hate me with cruel hatred" (Ps 25:19, KJV).

THOSE FAMILIAR with the psalms of David are aware of the many times he talked to God about his enemies. Sometimes he had in mind those tangible enemies of the battlefield, but more often David seems to be referring to spiritual enemies. Psalm 25 reveals that he knew he had spiritual heart trouble. "The troubles of my heart are enlarged" (v. 17, KJV). Christian believers today need this kind of spiritual sensitivity concerning their enemies.

The subject of aggressive spiritual warfare against the world, the flesh, and the devil is becoming increasingly important. Many are giving themselves to rampant abandonment and indulgence in fleshly sins. The glitter and appeal of the world system keeps pressuring for conformity. Satan and his kingdom relentlessly press their battle against believers and all of God's program. The purpose of this book is to help believers know biblical answers for handling our enemies.

The primary emphasis of this book is on practical spiritual instruction rather than theoretical exhortation. Christians need to know how to fight a good fight. The emphasis is upon the use of the objective, absolute truth of the Word of God, and not of subjective experience. Attributed to Martin Luther is this little quatrain which expresses well the thrust of this book:

> Feelings come and feelings go
> And feelings are deceiving;
> My warrant is the Word of God,
> Naught else is worth believing.

INTRODUCTION

BELIEVERS are being jolted awake to the reality of their participation in a spiritual warfare. This warfare promises to intensify as the return of our Lord draws nearer. The revival of interest in the varied forms of occultism is much more ominous than just another passing fad. Everything from the skyrocketing sales of Ouija boards to the open worship of Satan gives evidence of the increasing interest in exploring the supernatural. More rapidly than most of us realize, the questions people ask and the philosophies people believe are changing. No longer is the main debate of men concerned with whether you are a supernaturalist or a nonsupernaturalist. Today man's debate centers upon whether you are a "biblical supernaturalist," or an "investigating supernaturalist" who wants to experiment with occult phenomena or dabble in the various branches of sorcery and witchcraft. Numerous secular universities are now offering credited courses which study occult subject matter.

To counter this open involvement of the world with occult study, our Lord is raising up numerous authors to sound the alarm. Christian believers should welcome the increasing number of books which are being published by evangelical, Bible-believing Christians on the subject of Satan's kingdom and how it relates to Christian believers. Many of these books are listed in the bibliography of this book and are recommended for reading and study. Biblical studies on the ways and plans of Satan need to be prayerfully read by believers who are serious about their responsibility to "fight the good fight of faith" (1 Ti 6:12). The biblical doctrine concerning the fallen world of darkness deserves much more careful study than most believers have given it. Ignorance of Satan's devices leaves gaping holes in our defenses, through which the enemy is only too willing to move against us.

The purpose of this book is to approach the subject of spiritual warfare from a very practical viewpoint. It is my conviction that believers need to know what to do and how to proceed in their responsibility to "be strong in the Lord and in the power of His might" (Eph 6:10, KJV). They need to have usable tools at their disposal. They need to know how to proceed in getting free from the bondage of the devil and how to help others get free and stay free from a deflated, oppressed condition of demonic attack. If a Christian senses that his enemies are defeating him, he needs to know a step-by-step plan of how he can fight his way back to his rightful place of victory. The problem of Christians being tragically defeated by Satan is much more widespread than evangelicals have been willing to admit. Every pastor knows that the need for counseling among believers is one of the largest demands on his time. Many believers are hurting; they are frightened and confused. In desperation to help, too many pastors have approached such needs by taking a crash course in psychology, or by hurriedly referring the disturbed person to a psychologist or psychiatrist. Careful spiritual therapy may be the major need. Consideration must be given to the possibility of satanic or demonic defeat and bondage in the lives of such troubled believers. For too long the work of demons has been dismissed by most of us as a curious, vaguely understood phenomenon in animistic, heathen cultures, but it was not considered a problem which might invade our lives, our homes, our churches. Such willful ignorance of biblical teaching seems inexcusable and is long overdue for correction. The woeful lack of teaching and preaching on the subject of spiritual warfare during the last fifty years is in itself a testimony to the cleverness of the wiles of the

16

devil. Believers have all they need to defeat Satan's kingdom. Until recently, bold and aggressive attack upon the kingdom of darkness by believers who used the biblical weapons of our warfare had almost disappeared by default. To openly challenge intruding demons as did our Lord and the early disciples, was considered dangerous and far too extreme by most mainstream evangelicals. To hear of a missionary casting out demons sent chills of fear through most American Christians, who secretly thanked God that demon-possessed people were not here in America.

There are people all about us who are tormented and deeply troubled by the overt attacks of the powers of darkness against them. Several times each week I get calls from strangers desperate for some help. They have heard from some source that I am knowledgeable in the area of spiritual warfare, and almost like a drowning man reaching for something to grasp, they pour out their need. Just this morning a young man I have never met called and poured out his story. He is a college graduate, articulate, and displaying a large vocabulary. He is a professing Christian, yet he is in such emotional anguish and bondage that he cannot hold down a job. He has spent large sums of money on psychiatry without apparent help. His waking hours are torment, and his sleeping hours result in hideous, bizarre behavior and a trancelike condition. "What's wrong with me?" he cried out. "Am I possessed with demons?"

I suggested some steps for him to become aggressive in spiritual warfare, prayed with him, and referred him to a Christian layman who is helping folk in such need. I have seen the Lord Jesus Christ do wonders in setting such people free. The need for a practical handbook on spiritual warfare has become increasingly obvious to me. Sincere Christians need some tools of help which they can use to help themselves and others. It is with this need in mind that I have attempted to provide some of these tools in this book.

It is important that we keep a biblical balance in our warfare. We must be careful not to develop a "demon behind every bush" spiritual mentality. The old nature of man and its bent for evil, together with the world system, must be understood in biblical perspective.

It is the author's prayer that this book will help to change the defeating spirit of timidity and fearfulness that paralyzes so many believers and keeps them from warring a good warfare. The suggested practical helps given in the later chapters of this book have been proven in the author's own ministry and in the ministries of others, some of whom will be quoted in this book. May each reader take seriously the subject matter before him. This is not a topic for idle curiosity or trifling interest. There is too much at stake for us to be satisfied with anything less than being "mighty through God to the pulling down of strong holds" (2 Co 10:4, KJV).

1

THE BIBLICAL PERSPECTIVE OF WARFARE

"For we wrestle . . . against principalities, against powers, against the rulers of darkness of this world" (Eph
6:12).

"THE DEVIL MADE ME DO IT!" One hears that statement often
these days. Comedians, posters, bumper stickers, and
lapel pins keep the theme going. Most people laugh and
smile at this attempt of man to excuse himself of any guilt
in his sins. How man would like to laugh away the problem of sin and the misery and torment it often brings!

Such levity about Satan and his part in man's sins is
subtle satanic strategy against us. The prince of this world
sees to it that the world he controls laughs him off with
indifferent levity. Christians ought never to enter into
joke-making about Satan or hell. While believers do need
to exercise care in not assigning all of their wrongdoing as
Satan's responsibility, we must with biblical insight appreciate the awesome power of Satan's kingdom to influence us.

God's greatest servants have always shared an appreciation of the awesome power of Satan and his kingdom and
the complete victory over Satan's kingdom which is avail-

able to all believers through the mighty Person and work of our Lord Jesus Christ.

Jude warns us of apostate teachers who are "filthy dreamers," and part of whose folly is to "despise dominion, and speak evil of dignities" (Jude 8, KJV). He goes on to show how even Michael the archangel did not dare to judge Satan, but appealed to the Lord to rebuke him (v. 9).

Careful study of the epistles of Paul soon reveals the depth of understanding the Holy Spirit brought to the apostle concerning the need for wisely approaching spiritual warfare. The book of Ephesians is the New Testament handbook on spiritual warfare. Paul closes this epistle with a focus that seems to make successful spiritual warfare against Satan an important key to the message of the whole epistle. A believer's ability to enjoy the lofty spiritual benefits set forth in the first five-and-one-half chapters depends upon his being strong in the Lord and his effective warfare against Satan and his kingdom.

Martin Luther was also one who saw the need to enter into aggressive, biblically sound warfare against Satan and his kingdom. It is traditionally accepted that Luther so surely was aware of Satan's presence on one occasion that he threw his ink bottle at him. It is not difficult to believe such tradition when one sings the words of his great hymn, "A Mighty Fortress Is Our God."

> A mighty fortress is our God,
> A bulwark never failing;
> Our helper He, amid the flood
> Of mortal ills prevailing.
> > For still our ancient foe
> > Doth seek to work us woe;
> > His craft and power are great,
> > And, armed with cruel hate,
> On earth is not his equal.
>
> Did we in our own strength confide,
> Our striving would be losing,
> Were not the right Man on our side,
> The Man of God's own choosing.

Dost ask who that may be?
Christ Jesus, it is He;
Lord Sabaoth His name,
From age to age the same,
And He must win the battle.

And though this world, with devils filled,
Should threaten to undo us,
We will not fear, for God hath willed
His truth to triumph through us.
The prince of darkness grim—
We tremble not for him;
His rage we can endure,
For lo! his doom is sure,
One little word shall fell him

That word above all earthly powers—
No thanks to them — abideth;
The Spirit and the gifts are ours
Through Him who with us sideth.
Let goods and kindred go,
This mortal life also;
The body they may kill:
God's truth abideth still,
His kingdom is forever.

The believer's emphasis in spiritual warfare must be upon a biblical, doctrinal approach to the subject. Subjective feelings, emotional desires, and fervent sincerity are not sufficient weaponry against Satan. He yields no ground to emotion or sincerity. He retreats only from before the authority the believer has through his union with the Lord Jesus Christ and the absolute truth of the Word of God.

Many in the more feeling-oriented communions of believers are to be commended for their awareness of the need to see people loosed from Satan's bondage. However, if one might be permitted to exercise a note of loving concern, it has been my observation that far too many of these believers have substituted feelings, desire, and fervency of emotion in place of objective doctrinal truth. The defeat of our enemy depends on our reliance upon the Word of God and the Person and work of our Lord Jesus Christ.

The Word of God recognizes that we face three unique enemies which seek to defeat the spiritual life of believers. Commonly we speak of these three as the world, the flesh, and the devil. Each of these enemies has a unique and particular role to play in the warfare against believers. It is vital to our victory in the Lord Jesus Christ that we know how each of these enemies seeks to turn us aside from our purchased possession and position of victory. It is important for us to be able to discern what kind of temptation or testing we are facing in a given situation.

When a person becomes a believer in the Lord Jesus Christ, his relationship to everything in the physical, spiritual, mental, and emotional world undergoes a radical change. He is a new creation, and everything is becoming new. The believer is a citizen of heaven (Phil 3:20); he is God's child (Jn 1:12) and an heir of God. Believers are appointed to suffer with Christ and to be glorified together with Him (Ro 8:16-17).

Because of this new relationship to God, all believers are marked targets for attack from the same enemies that oppose and attack the Person, plans, and purposes of God. With such relentless plan of attack against us, believers must know all they can about their available defense system and their weapons of warfare.

Several years ago, while pastoring in Colorado, I witnessed the fascinating development of the beautiful new Air Force Academy near Colorado Springs. The US government purchased thousands of acres of land and then proceeded to pour multiplied millions of dollars into the construction of one of the most beautiful campuses in the world. Through a careful screening process, the US Air Force seeks to recruit the cream of American youth. For four years in a highly disciplined academic community, these gifted young men are trained and conditioned in the finest military tradition. Graduation day is just the beginning of many more long years of further training and preparation to defend our country and to prepare for military warfare. Our government demands that our military leaders spend their whole lifetime studying, improving, and perfecting military strategy.

The point begins to become obvious, doesn't it? If earthly military needs demand such study and careful preparation, how much more our preparation to meet our enemy demands our most diligent effort. The believer who does not become familiar with spiritual warfare will indeed be a poor soldier of Jesus Christ. The believer's enemies are engaged in unprecedented activity against him today. One's own observations, the entertainment industry, the mass media, numerous books by Christian authors, all sound the alarm. Christians are under concentrated attack today.

It is vital that I have doctrinal or biblical answers to such basic questions as: How do I recognize the world's attempt to press me into its mold, and how do I overcome the world? How do I defeat the works of my fleshly nature? How do I recognize temptations and testing from Satan and his demons, and what defeats these focused efforts to destroy me? Biblical answers to these questions will equip members of our Lord's body to walk in the spiritual health which has been supplied by their Head.

A number of years ago now, I led a young lady in her early twenties to a saving knowledge of the Lord Jesus Christ. She was radiant over her newfound joy and peace through the Lord Jesus Christ. Some very defeating sins and problems with nightmares and fears disappeared immediately. She was set free in Christ. Through neglect on my part and the young lady's own choice, however, adequate follow-up and careful grounding in the Word of God was not achieved. She lived some distance from the church, and after a few weeks, her attendance became very sporadic. Worldliness which had been a very prominent part of her life before her conversion continued. Fleshly sins were tolerated and excused with little concern.

After about a year had passed, this girl returned to my study for counseling. "It didn't last, Pastor," she said. "It was wonderful at first, but now my problems are much worse than before I received Christ. My nightmares are more hideous than ever, and I'm afraid all the time. I guess it just doesn't work for me."

This babe in Christ had become a tragic victim of her enemies. She did not know how to recognize and defeat the enemies which were out to destroy her spiritual victory and rob her of the enjoyment of God's will. Her experience abounds in the body of Christ today. The world, the flesh, and the devil must be challenged and defeated by the victory won for us through our Lord Jesus Christ.

2

WARFARE WITH THE FLESH

"To be fleshly minded is death; but to be spiritually minded is life and peace" (Ro 8:6, ASV).

A NEIGHBORHOOD BIBLE STUDY was in progress. The group was studying the book of Romans. A highly educated, professional man was asked to read from *The Living Bible* Romans 7:15-25:

> I don't understand myself at all, for I really want to do what is right, but I can't. I do what I don't want to — what I hate. I know perfectly well that what I am doing is wrong, and my bad conscience proves that I agree with these laws I am breaking. But I can't help myself, because I'm no longer doing it. It is sin inside me that is stronger than I am that makes me do these evil things.

At this point, his wife, who was in another part of the room, asked the lady next to her if her husband was making a confession. She recognized these words as so aptly describing her husband's struggles. She was assured that he was reading as he continued in the passage:

> I know I am rotten through and through so far as my old sinful nature is concerned. No matter which way I turn, I can't make myself do right. I want to but I can't. When I want to do good, I don't; and when I try not to do wrong, I do it anyway. Now if I am doing what I don't want to, it is plain where the trouble is: sin still has me in its evil grasp.

25

It seems to be a fact of life that when I want to do what is right, I inevitably do what is wrong. I love to do God's will so far as my new nature is concerned; but there is something else deep within me, in my lower nature, that is at war with my mind and wins the fight and makes me a slave to the sin that is still within me. In my mind I want to be God's willing servant but instead I find myself enslaved to sin.

So you see how it is: my new life tells me to do right, but the old nature that is still inside me loves to sin. Oh, what a terrible predicament I'm in! Who will free me from my slavery to this deadly lower nature? Thank God! It has been done by Jesus Christ our Lord. He has set me free.

The one doing this reading told me later that he just couldn't believe these words were in the Bible. He was sure that those leading the Bible study had deliberately chosen the passage for him to read. Being aggressive and vocal, he told them so, and they all had a good laugh over the incident.

How relevant the Word of God is. How pointedly it speaks to us about the experiences we are having.

Man has a depraved nature which presents a great challenge to any desire to do right. This depraved nature resulted from man's fall. Some would tell us that this debased, depraved nature is a holdover from man's primitive, savage, brute state. This evolutionary view of man rejects and is in contradiction to the Word of God which describes man as being created in the likeness and image of God on a plane only a little lower than God. "Yet Thou hast made him a little lower than God, And dost crown him with glory and majesty" (Ps 8:5, NASB).

Man's sinful nature did not arise out of his original constitution, nor was it a result of his environment. Man's sin nature resulted from his departure from God in an act of personal consciousness and deliberate, free will violation of God's holy law. The curse of man's willful sin resulted in a sinful nature, a disposition of the heart out of which sinful actions spring (Mt 15:19; Mk 7:21-23).

We have inherited this cursed sin nature from Adam (Ro 5:12-19). The law of inheriting our sin nature is the outworking of Adam's sin and the relationship of the human race to Adam as its head.

Evangelical Christians accept the fact that man inherits through the Fall a depraved human nature. This nature is opposed to God and is prone to sin. The Word of God uses several different words and phrases to describe this debased, weak, low tendency in man to be ungodly and sinful. For example, the "old man" describes what man was like before he receives Christ and becomes a "new man." (Ephesians 4:22, 24) The "natural man" describes this fallen condition as opposed to the "spiritual man." (1 Co 2)

One of the most common New Testament words used to identify man's fallen depraved nature is the word *flesh*. The word has several different usages in Scripture and does not always mean man's fallen nature. The context in which the word *flesh* appears usually makes unmistakably clear its usage or meaning.

Numerous New Testament passages depict for us the great struggle and warfare that the believer has with this fallen depraved nature. This is a battle the Christian faces completely apart from direct temptation from Satan or the powers of darkness. We must see that even though there is always a relationship between one enemy—our fallen nature—and the other—Satan—they are also separate. We must never underestimate the terrible strength of our fallen nature to hinder and destroy spiritual life and the holy life God desires us to live.

In such texts as that quoted from Romans 7, the apostle Paul recognized the total failure and depravity of our fallen, fleshly nature. The deadliness of this enemy is further expounded in Romans 8:7-8: "The [fleshly] mind is enmity against God: for it is not subject to the law of God, neither indeed can be. So then they that are in the flesh cannot please God" (KJV).

Romans 7:23 pictures this enemy of our flesh as being

the cause of an inner war, a struggle and a battle between the fallen nature and the new or spiritual nature that enters when we become believers and are born again (Jn 3:6-7).

While teaching a Sunday school class, I challenged the class to come up with a definition of the flesh as the Bible describes it. My own insight gained from the definition these believers shared: The flesh is a built-in law of failure, making it impossible for natural man to please or serve God. It is a compulsive inner force inherited from man's fall, which expresses itself in general and specific rebellion against God and His righteousness. The flesh can never be reformed or improved. The only hope for escape from the law of the flesh is its total execution and replacement by a new life in the Lord Jesus Christ.

One might find a more polished definition from an able theologian, but the practical insight of the deadly nature of the flesh seems to be captured here. The flesh cannot be tamed, reformed, or improved. It is so totally bad that it has to die. This terrible force is within us, and even after we have by faith counted him dead, he will attempt to spring to life again and control us.

Man's flesh, his fallen nature, has definite ways in which it tempts and wars against the spiritual man. The flesh is a deadly enemy which is capable of completely defeating a believer and keeping him from pleasing God with a holy life. One of the reasons the flesh is such a difficult enemy to handle is because of its close inner relationship to the believer's personality. The flesh is intimately intertwined with our mind, our will, and our emotions, and prior to his conversion, it pretty much controls a man's inner life.

It is important that a believer be able to identify the particular ways in which his flesh wars against him. Whenever one finds lists in the Scripture, they are worthy of careful study and analysis. The ways in which the flesh tempts us to sin are to be found in such a list in Galatians 5:19-21 (see also Mt 15:19; Mk 7:21-23). Successful spiritual warfare demands that the Christian become

familiar with such a list so that he can identify his temptation and apply the biblical remedy God has prescribed. If
our flesh is our problem, we'd better face it truthfully and
not try to lay the blame on Satan, the world, or some other
scapegoat. Unless we understand the source of the temta-
tion, we'll not know God's spiritual remedy to apply. The
list of fleshly sins and temptations mentioned in the
above-named passages seems to be intended to be fairly
comprehensive and complete. It would do us well to
memorize this list of fleshly sins so that we could quickly
identify the kind of temptation which is working against
us.

Let's look at the list Galatians 5 presents. The text opens
with the bold statement: "Now the works of the flesh are
manifest, which are these" (v. 19, KJV). The apostle, by the
guidance of the Holy Spirit, is listing as to how the flesh is
going to work against us and war against the regenerate
spirit of man. The first of the listing specifies moral sins of
a sensual, sexual nature and then moves on into areas that
cause conflicts and troubles of a very grave nature.

Adultery (cf. Mt 15:19; Mk 7:21). This refers to thoughts
or acts of immorality after marriage. Adultery springs from
the selfish, fleshly desire for physical gratification without
spiritual responsibility. Adultery expresses rebellion of
the flesh against God's law of purity and strikes at the
sacredness of marriage (Heb 13:4).

Fornication (cf. Mk 7:21). This fleshly sin is the violation of God's moral law before marriage. Fornication
springs from the fleshly desire to gratify sensual appetites
without marriage responsibility and the necessity of God's
approval. There is no place or excuse for fornication in
God's plan (1 Co 6:13, 18).

Uncleanness (cf. Mk 7:21). This fleshly sin includes a
wide range of moral sins. Evil or impure thoughts, so-
called dirty stories, lustful desires, desires to read pornography or to see morally unclean pictures or movies would
certainly be included. Uncleanness springs from the
fleshly desire to gratify sensual appetite through thoughts

and words in conflict with God's holy nature and divine plan.

Lasciviousness (cf. Mk 7:22). This sin represents the practice of stirring up lustful desires which cannot be satisfied within the limits of God's approval. One may be lascivious about his dress, his speech, his laughter, his smile, his eyes, his physical gestures, his modesty, and so forth. This sin springs from the fleshly desire to attract attention to one's self in a manner that flaunts God's standards of moral purity.

Idolatry. This sin is the flesh rebelling against worshiping only the true and living God. Idolatry takes place when we physically or mentally put anything before God. Pleasure, money, things, our work, even our families may become gods. This fleshly sin springs from our desire to choose the god that pleases our flesh rather than bowing before the true and living God.

Witchcraft. This sin of the flesh springs from our desire to contact and relate to the mysterious spirit world. In rebellious curiosity, we desire to learn the mysteries of the unseen world in a manner other than that revealed by God in His Word. This fleshly sin of witchcraft includes the whole occult realm. Ouija boards, tarot cards, seances, spiritism, levitation, astrology, the pendulum, and such like are tools of this sin. It is interesting that the Greek word translated witchcraft or sorcery in our English texts is the word *pharmakia*, from which we get our English word *pharmacy*, referring to drugs. The use of drugs for sensational, mind-expanding experience is a form of sorcery. Drug experimentation is a fleshly sin which leads on into deeper bondage with Satan's kingdom.

Hatred. This fleshly sin expresses itself in dark, ugly feelings of bitterness, contempt, and loathing of another person. Hatred springs from the fleshly desire to establish one's worth apart from God's plan of salvation. This sin strikes out at God's demand that we forgive one another and leave all vengeance to God.

Variance or quarreling. This fleshly sin expresses itself

as we become a part of strife and discord. This sin springs from the fleshly desire for attention and the compulsion to prove that we are right.

Emulations or jealousy. This fleshly sin expresses itself in inner feelings of resentment that someone else is or has what we want. Jealousy springs from the fleshly desire for self-attention above interest in others. It also manifests a lack of self-acceptance and thankfulness to God that **He** made us just as He wants us.

Wrath. This means a bad temper, violent anger, or raging resentment. Anger or wrath springs from a desire of the flesh to strike out at anything that threatens self interests. Anger is the attempt of the flesh to step in and take vengeance out of God's hands.

Strife. Strife is self-seeking rivalry. This fleshly sin springs from a selfish desire to pull down others who in any way threaten us. It strikes out against God's love for all men; a love so great that "while we were yet sinners, Christ died for us" (Ro 5:8, KJV).

Seditions. This word literally means to divide, to split in two parts. This fleshly sin springs from a selfish desire to identify with a group who will support my selfish interests. This fleshly indulgence is what causes church splits and factions of quarreling among believers. The apostle Paul rebuked the Corinthians for this kind of indulging in fleshly sin. The spirit of sedition strikes at the essential unity of the body of Christ and divides that which by the work of Christ and the grace of God is made one.

Heresies. Much like seditions, this fleshliness is a party spirit of unbiblical teaching which divides believers over nonessentials. This sin springs from a fleshly desire to support conduct with doctrinal argument. This has been one of the fleshly sins which many leaders of fundamental believers have become subtly guilty. This sin strikes at God's gift of love and His command not to engage in foolish questions which create strife (2 Ti 2:23).

Envyings. This sin describes an inner discontent as we look upon another's success or superiority with a desire

31

for his place. Envy springs from a lack of inner security and trust that God will enable us to have and achieve just what He wants us to have. Envy is a refusal to be satisfied with God's gift of His grace to us.

Murders (cf. Mt 15:19; Mk 7:21). Satan is a murderer, but the human heart full of hatred and wrath is capable of murder, too. The sin of murder expresses the rebellious desire of the flesh to remove even a life that stands in the way of some self-gratifying goal.

Drunkenness. This fleshly sin would include reliance upon all intoxicants such as alcohol and drugs, to produce an artificial means of escape from facing our sins and responsibilities. This fleshliness springs from a desire to create a sense of well being. It strikes at the work of the Holy Spirit who convicts man of his sins and creates guilt and conviction designed to bring man to faith and repentance. Drunkenness seeks by a fleshly stimulation to produce a sense of well being which in truth and permanency can only be produced by the fullness of the Holy Spirit (Eph 5:18).

Reveling and such like. This fleshliness expresses itself in orgies, carousings, and general sensual escapism. This sin brings others into the sins of the flesh with us and often leads into group sensual involvement. Revelings lead people into a type of conduct where their sensual appetites dictate their behavior. This sin springs from man's desire to gratify his body and soulish appetites without moral responsibility. Such fleshliness strikes at God's moral law and man's very creation as a spirit being which is planned of God to rule his soul and body.

Verse 21 of Galatians 5 points out that those who are doing these sins in continual practice are not those who will inherit God's kingdom. These are the sins of the natural man who has never been born again. Believers have been delivered from these fleshly sins through Christ's death on the cross and His resurrection. Now we are responsible to claim our position of victory over them.

Let us hasten to point out that warfare with our flesh is a

lifetime warfare which we must meet. John Knox, the great Scottish reformer, was one of God's noblest servants and one of the most deeply spiritual men the world has ever known. In the year he died, John Knox wrote these words in his "Answer to a Letter of James Lurie, a Scottish Jesuit." He wrote,

> Lord Jesus, receive my spirit, and put an end at Thy good pleasure to this my miserable life; for justice and truth are not to be found among the sons of men . . . . Be merciful unto me, O Lord. . . . Now after many battles, I find nothing in me but vanity and corruption. For in quietness I am negligent, in trouble impatient, tending to desperation; . . . pride and ambition assault me on the one part, covetousness and malice trouble me on the other; briefly, Oh Lord, the affections of the flesh do almost suppress the operation of Thy Spirit. . . . In none of the aforesaid I do delight; but I am troubled, and that sore against the desire of my inward man which sobs for my corruption, and would repose in Thy mercy alone; to which I claim, and that in the promise that Thou hast made to all penitent sinners of whose number I profess myself to be one.*

Thus, at the very close of his life, John Knox, the mighty man of prayer and virtue, who claimed Scotland for God, was yet facing warfare with his flesh. He also reveals in the above words of repentance and trust in the Lord that he pressed the battle against his flesh in spiritual warfare. He was aggressive against his fallen nature.

Earlier in his life he wrote his "Treatise on Prayer," in which he referred to his days as a galley slave as punishment for his reform preaching. He said,

> I know how hard the battle is between the flesh and the spirit under the heavy cross of affliction, when no worldly defense but present death doth appear. I know the grudging and murmuring complaints of the flesh, I know the anger, wrath and indignation it conceiveth against God, calling all His promises in doubt, and being ready every

*Bessie G. Olson, *John Knox-A Great Intercessor*, Hall of Fame Series (Des Moines: Walfred, 1956), pp. 45-46.

hour utterly to fall from God against which rests only faith, provoking us to call earnestly, and pray for assistance of God's Spirit, wherein, if we continue, our most desperate calamities shall He turn to gladness and a prosperous end.†

One can certainly read shades of Romans 7 and 8 into the experiences of John Knox as he battled the flesh and tasted the victory of the Spirit. Such strong warfare with the flesh are the experiences of all God's saints. The more one grows into spiritual maturity and the riches of grace, the more his warfare with the flesh becomes defined and focused in intensity.

Why is warfare with the flesh so important? This is a much deeper and more important question than it first appears. The spiritual wrongness of the sins of the flesh is obvious. Each dishonors God. Each strikes at God's right to direct and discipline our lives. Each fleshly sin flows out of the corrupt old man's depravity and is in direct confrontation of the conduct of the new man.

Yet even beyond these more obvious dangers of indulging in fleshly sins lies a more subtle and deadly danger. Ephesians 4 deals with the sins of the flesh in the context of the old man (v. 22) and the new man (v. 24). In this context, suddenly the apostle Paul warns, "Neither give place to the devil" (v. 27, KJV). This warning indicates that through the believer exercising his will to commit these fleshly sins, he gives place—literally claim or practical ground—to Satan's activity in his life. Giving way willfully to practice sins of the flesh gives occasion for Satan to have his way in a believer's life. Although all legal claim of Satan against us was canceled at the cross, a believer's willful indulgence in fleshly sins gives the enemy a place or a claim against us which he will be quick to exploit.

This possibility of satanic involvement in a believer's life is alluded to in many other New Testament passages. To Timothy, the apostle Paul wrote of the need to instruct those who are in fleshly sins of strife and opposing them-

†Ibid., p. 12.

selves with the trust that God may grant repentance to them. He warns that those who practice such fleshly sins come into the snare of the devil and are "taken captive by him at his will" (2 Ti 2:26, KJV, cf. vv. 22-26). Although there are some interpreters who feel that this passage does not refer to true believers, I believe that the apostle meant it to be a sober warning to all men that careless, fleshly living means we are entering Satan's territory. Fleshly-living believers certainly can come into a state of bondage to Satan where they are living in accord with Satan's will rather than the will of God. That is a fairly obvious reality, in harmony with the whole tenure of Scripture and its emphasis upon man's responsibility.

This rather sobering observation, then, indicates that willful indulgence in fleshly sins without claiming our ground of victory in the Lord Jesus Christ can produce a bondage to Satan. There comes a time where the practice of a particular fleshly sin may move from a sin of the flesh into a sin controlled and dictated by satanic, demonic activity. This means that the compulsive inner desire of the old nature is joined by a strong spirit of demonic power that begins to dictate in a given area the behavior of that believer. Once spiritual wickedness has gained a foothold in a life, it seeks to go on to develop a whole hierarchy of powers of darkness against that person's life. More will be discussed of this phenomena of spiritual warfare in later chapters, but suffice its mention here to sober us to the urgent need for victory over our flesh. Failure to claim our Lord's provided victory will lead on to deeper and more serious warfare and defeat.

How do I overcome the flesh? Most Christians readily admit their battle with the fleshly sins as listed in Galatians 5. Indulgence in the sins of the flesh spells great misery for sinner and saint alike. The worldling who yields to his old nature's appetites may well experience the tragedy of some skid row. Yielding to the sins of the flesh always leads any believer far afield of the will of God for his life. Indulging in fleshly sin may cause one to be so

35

preoccupied with the pride of position, the acquiring of possessions, or the pursuit of pleasure that his life focuses only on self-centered concerns. There are three steps to victory over the flesh which are set forth in Galatians 5 and in other New Testament teaching upon this enemy.

The first step is a walk of honesty (Mk 7:21-23; Gal 5:17-21). It should be obvious to us all that one of the reasons for a listing of such fleshly sins or sins of our sinful heart as appear in the Word is the importance of being honest with ourselves. We do not all face temptation from each of these sins in equal degree. One may have little problem with temptations to be impure while facing a real battle with jealousy or anger. Another may face little problem with jealousy but have a terrible defeat when it comes to a temptation toward drunkenness and reveling. Someplace in this listing of fleshly sins, each believer is going to see himself. This is just what the Holy Spirit wants. He wants us to be honest. He wants us to see and admit our old depraved fleshly nature. He wants us daily aware that the old man must die. God is never in the business of reforming natural man. God only regenerates and makes us new creatures. Some believers stay in the business of trying to reform their old nature. It disturbs them that they continue to see such a potential for evil within them. Yet one of the most essential prerequisites to a victorious Christian life is to see and know the old nature in its depraved failure. We must give up totally any thought of ever reforming this old depraved nature.

Thus a first important step to victory over the flesh is the capacity to be honest. We must see and admit the fleshly sins which are our peculiar temptation and defeat. Do not try to gloss over them. Do not try to hide them from yourself and others or try to convince God they are not really there. Rather, it is important to ask the Holy Spirit to show you your fleshly sins in all of their lurid ugliness. Until there is such honesty, you will just go on being the victim of your flesh and will be giving ground to Satan. God is very convinced of our depravity and the sins of our flesh, and He wants us to be just as convinced. This is important before we will be willing to take the next step.

The second step in gaining victory over the flesh is a walk of death (Ro 6:1-13; Gal 2:20; 5:24). "And they that are Christ's have crucified the flesh with the affections and lusts" (Gal 5:24, KJV). "Likewise reckon ye also yourselves to be dead indeed unto sin, but alive unto God through Jesus Christ our Lord" (Ro 6:11, KJV).

Spiritual warfare in any of its victories is achieved through objective fact and not through subjective feelings. This point will be stressed often in these pages. Faith always proceeds on the basis of absolute truth and not vague wishes and emotional desires.

War against our flesh must proceed on the basis of truth and the appropriation of truth, and not on the untrustworthy basis of feeling. A fact of history is that the Lord Jesus Christ died on the cross of Calvary. He died there bearing our sins in His own body. He that knew no sin, became sin for us. This is absolute fact declared true by the Word of God. It is also a fact that in a very real sense because of the substitutionary nature of Christ's death that His death was our death. When a person believes on the Lord Jesus, he is baptized by the Holy Spirit into the death of Jesus Christ (Ro 6:3-6). He is united with the Lord Jesus Christ in His death. He has no other ground to claim as his right to enter through salvation's door and into the presence of God than the fact that full payment was made in the death of Christ for his sin. His death, the punishment for his sin, took place in the death of the Lord Jesus Christ. This is objective fact; apart from this truth no one can claim victory over his sin nature.

Romans 6:6 states clearly what my union with the death of Christ did to my sin nature. "For we know that our old self was crucified with him so that the body of sin might be rendered powerless, that we should no longer be slaves to sin—because anyone who has died has been freed from sin."

The believer's sin nature was crucified with Christ not

37

only to pay the debt his sin deserved, but also to render powerless that sin nature so the believer would no longer have to be held in its control. The believer's inherited, depraved sin nature was crucified with Christ at Calvary so he would no longer have to be slave to sin.

Overcoming fleshly sins in subjective experience now necessitates that a person reckon [better, "appropriate"] himself dead unto sin through Jesus Christ (see Ro 6:11). Victory over the flesh is always an active, aggressive, day-to-day and moment-by-moment appropriation of the absolute truth that "I have been crucified with Christ" (Gal 2:20).

It is a joyful moment indeed when a believer actively participates in the death of the old man. After admitting the depravity and wickedness of the flesh in honesty before God, it is necessary to see that the only thing to do with this old nature is to let it die. We must appropriate its death, which took place on the cross. Now the question arises in a very practical way as to how that is done. Here is a practical prayer expression of the daily appropriation of our death with Christ which accomplished our victory over the flesh:

Heavenly Father, I enter by faith today into death with the Lord Jesus Christ on the cross. I appropriate all of the benefit of the crucifixion which is mine because of my union with Christ. I count myself dead to my old fleshly nature and all of its workings through my union with Christ at the cross. I recognize that my old nature always wants to resurrect itself against You and Your will for my life, but I will to let it remain dead in death with my Lord on the cross. I am thankful that this absolute truth can be my subjective experience. I recognize that appropriating the death of my flesh is an essential step to victory over these fleshly temptations which buffet me. Amen.

I believe it to be very important to keep this objective truth constantly in the forefront of our daily living of the Christian life. Our hope of victory over our fleshly sins is only in the appropriation by faith of our death to these sins with Christ.

The third step is a walk in the Spirit (Ro 6:11; Gal 5:16-25). For the flesh to be conquered, death is not enough; new life must enter into our beings. We are also to reckon ourselves alive unto God, as well as dead unto sin (see Ro 6:11). It is obvious that we must not leave a vacuum within ourselves as we appropriate our death to the old man. We must be filled with newness of life.

Another objective fact we must see and act upon is that the Lord Jesus Christ rose from the dead. This is absolute truth, even though Satan and critics have assailed this truth. It still stands as immutable fact and follows as objective fact that all believers are united with Christ in His resurrection. Just as Christ arose from His death, so it is true that we are risen with Him. We have newness of life in Him. Yet, it again remains for us to appropriate our new life (Ro 6:4-5).

The moment we believe, the Holy Spirit baptizes us into Christ. We are united with Christ by this work of the Holy Spirit, and through this union we are made to be partakers of the resurrection life of our Lord (Ro 6:5, 8).

This newness, this resurrection life of Christ, is brought into our experience as the Person of the Holy Spirit is granted fullness of control. The Holy Spirit enters all believers' lives the moment we believe and are saved (Jn 3:6; Ro 8:9, 10). We must not doubt this objective fact. To doubt or disbelieve the indwelling presence of the Holy Spirit within our spirit is to believe the lie of Satan and be deceived.

It does remain the believer's responsibility to be filled with the Spirit (Eph 5:18). This is another way of saying that we must appropriate or act upon the truth that the Holy Spirit lives within us. We are composite beings yet functioning in an essential unity. We have a body, a soul, and a spirit. Our soul contains our personality, which is made up of our mind, our will, and our emotion. When one speaks of being "filled with the Spirit" it means that his body, his soul, and his spirit are controlled and directed by the enabling grace of the Holy Spirit. The new life which is his in the fact of the resurrection of Christ enters into the total, the fullness of his being.

Much discussion abounds today, what with the popular and growing charismatic emphasis upon the baptism of the Holy Spirit. Many differing views abound as to how and when this experience comes to the believer. It is not the purpose of this book to make an extended study of the Person and work of the Holy Spirit, but I do believe it important to warn against seeking mystical experiences with the Holy Spirit which one could subjectively refer to as the time when he was baptized with the Spirit. Keep in mind that the apostle Paul makes the baptism of the Spirit an objective fact by which believers are made members of the body of Christ (1 Co 12:13). Subjective feelings or experiences are not a safe ground for interpreting what one has received from the Holy Spirit. Satan is an able and subtle imitator of God's work, and he is never more deceiving than in the area of feelings and experiences. Through his myriads of spirit beings, he is capable of imitating and giving feelings and experiences which may be very similar to the feelings which may accompany the work of the Holy Spirit. Numerous people have come to me under bondage to some dark power of Satan who were brought under that bondage while seeking an experience with the Holy Spirit which they could interpret to be the baptism of the Holy Spirit.

I had this danger brought home to my own life in a very vivid personal experience back in the early days of my ministry. On an occasion when I was spending a prolonged period in prayer for the delivery of a certain message, I felt led to plead with God for the empowering of my life and the anointing of the Holy Spirit upon me to enable me to speak His Word with power. On that occasion God answered with a most wonderful experiential moving upon me. God's presence seemed to flow over me like a warming, scintillating breath. Feelings flowed through

40

my body like a gentle, quickening charge. Many who have sought a deeper touch from God in prayer have testified to similar experiences at times. After that time with the Lord, I spoke with unusual power and unction on that occasion.

A problem arose in my life, however, when I began to find myself seeking such an experience as an evidence of God's anointing almost every time I was called upon to speak. I can recall one such occasion when the results after the feelings had been there were discouraging indeed. The message had been delivered with great difficulty and a complete lack of liberty. I began to ask the Lord why. It was revealed through meditating on the Word that I was beginning to function on feeling and experience rather than upon fact and faith. I was impressed to see that when Satan draws near, the emotional and feeling responses of the body can be very similar to what had been experienced in the Holy Spirit's presence. Eliphaz, Job's friend, testifies to this fact in Job 4:15 when he states, "Then a spirit passed before my face; the hair of my flesh stood up" (KJV).

The first time I read those words after the experience just related, I saw how my experience was similar to that of Eliphaz. The supernatural presence of any powerful spirit being can and often does precipitate some unusual body and soul feelings and sensations in us mortals. Those who have attended seances and other spiritualist meetings testify to such fact.

The point of this observation is to emphasize strongly that we must not depend upon feeling and experience as an evidence of our being filled with the Holy Spirit. Even the so-called experience of speaking in tongues must be exercised with much care. Whenever anyone tells me that he speaks in an unknown tongue and that this is an evidence of the fact that he has been filled with the Spirit, as kindly as I can I ask him if he has tested the spirit. The Holy Spirit tells us to do this in 1 John 4:1-4. He will not be insulted by such a test. If you speak in an unknown tongue, I urge you to obey this instruction of the Spirit. While using a tongue, your own mind must be largely inactive. In your mind you can command the spirit behind the tongue to answer clearly with an answer to your mind, "Has Jesus Christ come in the flesh? Is Jesus Christ Lord?" Insist upon a clear definite affirmative yes. The Holy Spirit will always respond with a praising yes. Another spirit may well respond with some evasive answer or even a very blunt no. I know of cases where such testing has revealed the invasion of a wicked spirit into the experience of believers.‡

The filling of the spirit must thus rest upon objective fact and not upon subjective feelings. The filling of the Holy Spirit is to be appropriated by faith. The following outline presents a biblical procedure for obeying the command to be filled with the Spirit.

A. Engage in an honest inner examination (Ac 20:28). It is important to be open and honest with God about yourself.

B. Confess all known sin (1 Jn 1:9). Verbalizing one's transgressions is very important. If our sins have wronged others, it is important to also ask that person's forgiveness. It is a spiritually right and helpful thing to go to another person and say, "I was wrong for having lied to you. I'm asking you to forgive me. Will you please forgive me?" In confession of sins it is also helpful to take back from Satan any ground which he has tried to assume against you because of yielding to a particular sin (Eph 4:27).

C. Yield yourself to God (Ro 6:13). As an act of your own will, yield all areas of your life over to God. Your business life, entertainment life, social life, home life, thought life, all must be yielded to the Lord's authority and control. This includes obedience to the Word of God which is the Spirit's Word.

D. Express your desire for the Holy Spirit to fill you (Lk 11:13; Eph 5:18).

E. Believe you are filled (Ro 14:23). Act by faith and not by feeling. Take God at His Word.

‡For an excellent discussion of this subject, see Ernest B. Rockstad, *Speaking in Other Tongues and the Fullness of the Holy Spirit* (Andover, Kan.: Rockstad, n.d.).

F. Continue to obey God's revealed will as expressed in the Scriptures. Many well-meaning Christians interpret obeying the Lord as some sort of inner light or a mystical confidence that whatever they do when they think they are filled by the Spirit is right and unassailable. The Holy Spirit never leads us to disobey the Holy Word He inspired. He will never lead us to believe anything or to engage in activity or behavior which is contrary to God's revealed will expressed in the Scriptures.

A walk in the Spirit is absolutely essential if we are to know victory over the flesh. Let me suggest again a daily prayer which may suggest a practical way of appropriating this walk in the Spirit, which not only produces victory over the flesh and its sin manifestations, but also the fruit of the Spirit—"love, joy, peace, patience, kindness, goodness, faithfulness, gentleness, self-control" (Gal 5:22-23):

Blessed heavenly Father, in the name of the Lord Jesus Christ I desire to walk in the Spirit today. I recognize that only as He lives the life of the Lord Jesus Christ in me will I be able to escape the works of my flesh. I desire the Holy Spirit to bring all of the work of the crucifixion and the resurrection of Christ into my life today. I pray that the Holy Spirit may produce His fruit within my whole being and shed abroad in my heart great love for the heavenly Father, for the Lord Jesus Christ, and for others about me. Forgive me, dear Holy Spirit, for all times I have grieved or quenched You. Enable me to respond to Your grace and to be sensitive to Your voice. Grant to me the desire and enablement to be obedient to Your precious Word. Grant me discernment to avoid being deceived by false spirits. I desire that the Holy Spirit fill all of my being with His presence and control me by faith. I trust my victory over the flesh today completely into the hands of the Holy Spirit as I let Him take control of me. In the name of the Lord Jesus Christ, I receive all the fullness of the Holy Spirit into all areas of my being today. Amen.

We must not lose sight of the importance of verbalizing sound doctrine. A chapter is devoted to this subject later in this book, but let me stress it here as it relates to the defeat of our flesh. The only victory we have over the flesh is that which God has provided and we appropriate.

3

WARFARE WITH
THE WORLD

"May I never boast except in the cross of our Lord Jesus Christ, through which the world has been crucified to me, and I to the world" (Gal 6:14).

HE CAME INTO MY STUDY one day with a very apprehensive look on his face. His hand was wet with perspiration as I shook it, betraying deep inner anxiety. I didn't know him well, but I knew he was a Christian. "I just had to talk to someone," he confided. "I'm all torn up inside."

As we talked, he revealed that he was having a great battle against moral uncleanness. Our conversation proceeded along this line. "I really want to be morally clean," he declared, "but everywhere I go I'm bombarded by moral filth. Pornography confronts me at every newsstand, magazine rack, and book counter. X-rated movies constantly arouse my curiosity, and I just can't resist going. I hate myself when I do but I just can't handle all of this available filth. Pastor, what am I to do? Can you help me?"

This man was experiencing a battle with his flesh which was greatly aggravated by the world system. This world is no longer the natural habitat for men who have been born again. The Christian is a citizen of heaven, and this world's system runs counter to his high calling. "But our citizenship is in heaven. And we eagerly await a Savior from there, the Lord Jesus Christ" (Phil 3:20).

How do we deal with the world as our enemy? How do we even know what the world is? The world is very clearly defined in Scripture as an active enemy of believers. It is an enemy which we are to be aggressively against in our spiritual warfare. The Holy Spirit gives believers the imperative command: "Love not the world, neither the things that are in the world. If any man love the world, the love of the Father is not in him" (1 Jn 2:15, KJV). The Lord Jesus reminded His disciples: "If ye were of the world, the world would love his own; but because ye are not of the world, but I have chosen you out of the world, therefore the world hateth you" (Jn 15:19, KJV).

There are three Greek words which are sometimes translated from the Greek into the English by the word *world*. The Greek word *oikoumene* is commonly used to signify the populated world or the earth we live upon. The word *aion* is sometimes translated "world" but more often should be translated "age," meaning the age of time in which we live (Ro 12:2; 2 Co 4:4; Gal 1-4). Sometimes this word is meant to describe the philosophy or system of thought which characterizes a particular age and in that sense is an enemy to be overcome. In such instances, *aion* is almost interchangeable in meaning with our next word, *kosmos*.

The main Greek word used to describe our enemy, the world, is the word *kosmos*. The main usage of this word describes the order or system that runs this inhabited earth. It is a spiritual system of things that is opposed to God and the Lord Jesus Christ. The word *kosmos* is very complex and difficult to define. In John 3:16 God is declared to love this world (*kosmos*), but in 1 John 2:15 believers are specifically commanded to not love the world (*kosmos*). The context has to tell us in such cases what is meant by the usage of the word *world* or *kosmos*.

46

Sometimes it may mean the earth or the physical world; at other times the world of human beings or, more common, the whole world system over which Satan rules (Jn 12:31; 1 Jn 5:19). As our enemy, the world is the whole organized system, made up of varying and changing social, economic, materialistic, and religious philosophies which have their expression through the organizations and personalities of human beings. The world system in its function is a composite expression of the depravity of man and the intrigues of Satan's rule, combining in opposition to the soverign rule of God.

Warren Wiersbe, in his book *Be Real*, points out that we often use the word *world* in the sense of system in our daily conversation. The TV announcer says, "We bring you the news from the world of sports." "The world of sports" is not a separate planet or continent. It is an organized system, made up of a set of ideas, people, activities, purposes; it is the system that keeps things going.*

The world that is our enemy as believers is this *kosmos,* this system which is opposed to all that believers are to love and support, namely the work of our Lord Jesus Christ upon this earth.

The question arises as to why this world system is so wrong and why it is such an enemy to resist and reject. There are two good reasons why the world is such a deadly enemy. The world system seems to be best understood as an extension of man's two very real enemies. Both Satan and man's flesh or old nature have a vital part in formulating the world system in its activities and philosophies. The apostle John makes clear that "all that is in the world, the lust of the flesh, and the lust of the eyes, and the pride of life, is not of the Father, but is of the world" (1 Jn 2:16, KJV). This text would certainly support that the world contains much in its system that is an extension, a larger expression, of man's depraved inner nature. Its deadliness as an enemy is seen when we look at the vicious circle of problems for man it is capable of creating. Man, by his

*Warren W. Wiersbe, *Be Real* (Wheaton, Ill.: Victor, 1972), p. 66.

fallen nature, has an inner compulsive problem with "adultery, fornication, uncleanness, lasciviousness, idolatry, witchcraft, hatred, variance, emulations, wrath, strife, seditions, heresies, envyings, drunkenness, revelings and such like" (Gal 5:19-21, KJV). The problem man has, however, begins to intensify when the world system as an extension of man's fleshliness begins to provide an atmosphere, a climate, a system which promotes these fleshly sins. The world system begins to surround man with that which intensifies the inner problem he already has as a fallen creature. One never cures a man's problem by surrounding him with that which feeds his problem. An alcoholic cannot cure his drunkenness with all the liquor he wants to drink. An immoral person cannot resolve his problem by reading pornography and engaging in immoral conduct. Yet this is precisely what the world does for depraved man; it surrounds him with that which his flesh desires.

The world system also includes and is an extension of Satan's warfare against God's plans for the believer. The Lord Jesus Christ called Satan the prince of this world (Jn 12:31). First John 5:19 states: "We know that we are of God, and the whole world lies in the power of the evil one" (NASB).

Satan has a very highly organized kingdom that seeks to rule over the world system. The apostle Paul defines this highly structured kingdom which makes a strong impact upon the world in Ephesians 6:11-12, which we will look at in some detail a little later in this book. Satan, through his wiles and evil spirits, seeks to manipulate and rule over the whole world system. His showing our Lord all the kingdoms of the world with their glory and then promising to give them to Him if He would worship Satan was a real temptation. One must conclude that Satan's rule over the world is very much a part of the picture of our warfare.

The world system is marked by many of Satan's most vicious attacks against God and against the believer's faith. All of the ways Satan tempts men can be seen as a part of the world system. Satan tempts us to question God's Word; and in the world system we can see much of this questioning.

On a recent occasion we enjoyed a family outing to the zoo. Surely that would be harmless in the world system. Yet as we walked through this zoo and enjoyed the animals of God's creation, we saw countless numbers of references to the theory of evolution stated as if it were proven fact. The world, even in a zoo, was doing Satan's work of getting us to question God's Word.

Sometimes Christians think of worldliness as being a few questionable amusements and doubtful practices. Sometimes believers are called worldly Christians only if they attend the movies, go to dances, play cards, smoke, or engage in some other frowned-upon activity. Yet worldliness is more than this. Worldliness is a matter of heart attitude. Believers may refrain from doing any doubtful practices and yet be very worldly. At any time the world system causes us to think or act contrary to God's will, then we've fallen into its trap and have become worldly.

The world has specific ways in which it tempts the believer to sin and disobey God's will. As we have already seen, the world system may provide us with many varied enticements to the sins of the flesh or direct activities or pronouncements that tempt us as Satan does. We should never be surprised to see the world advertising or propagating some program or philosophy that is just like what Satan himself would try to bring to us.

Yet perhaps it would be good for us to look at some of the world's unique pressures on believers which are beyond its being an extension department of the temptations of the flesh and Satan.

The world tempts us to gain its treasure and seek its approval (Lk 9:23-25). The world system seeks to tempt us to gain or seek its power, its position, and its honor that we might be exalted in the world. Our Lord warns that even if we gained the whole world we'd have no advantage because we'd lose ourselves in the process.

The world tempts us to be ashamed of the Lord Jesus Christ (Lk 9:26, cf. Ro 10:11). The world system exalts its own intellectual system and rejects God's truth as foolishness (1 Cor 1:18-31). The world tempts believers to conform to the world's standards (Jn 15:18-19; Jn 17:6, 9, 14-16; Ro 12:2; Col 2:8). The world system tries to dictate our values, to pressure us into its mold. Modern day communications and media put a tremendous pressure upon believers in the western world to conform to its standards. Governments, television, educational systems, the press, music, literature, art, interaction with the people in our work and leisure, and virtually everything in our society can bring the world's pressure to tempt us to step out of God's will.

Our family is seeking to love and help a very beautiful and lovely girl twenty-two years of age. She has, however, a staggering problem. She is a hard line drug addict. Since she was sixteen she has used drugs profusely. She was reared in a well-to-do family in one of Chicago's finest suburbs. She had every advantage the world could offer her. Her talents of music, art, and ice skating were developed to a degree of unusual excellence. She still plays the piano with a feeling and beauty seldom heard. Yet here she is, a widow at twenty-two years of age. Her husband died last July of an overdose of drugs. She has been in and out of hospitals for treatment of varied overdoses and for attempts to detoxify her and see her set free from drugs. Up until this time, she has always reverted to her drug pattern. She cannot possibly care for her three-year-old daughter. Her great gifts and intelligence are wasted on the streets of the city in a vain search for enough drugs to numb her pain. Brokenhearted parents have tried all they know to do, but their best efforts have only cost them multiplied thousands of dollars without any evident help. What's the matter? What caused this girl's painful condition? Certainly the flesh must have had a part in her problem, particularly in those early days. Satan must also be working to hold this one for whom Christ died in his bondage.

Yet the principal enemy that has contributed the most to her agony seems to be the world. The world's value system has warped her objectives and goals. The world's raucous music has corrupted her mind and emotions. The world's system of justice has permitted her to freely acquire drugs from pushers out on bail. The world's careless indifference toward the treatment of drug victims lets her problem go on and on. The world's method of treating drug victims provides no spiritual values. The world system of corruption and graft that permits the drug traffic to operate makes her a necessary consumer. On and on go the problems the world has created and continues to foster.

There is only one hope for this dear girl. Only the victory God has provided over the world, the flesh, and the devil will ever see her delivered. She has made a profession of faith, and even though the problem isn't yet solved, I believe that God is going to bring her through to victory. How, as a believer, will she handle the world's temptations? Certainly she, like so many others who have been saved out of such a life, will face great battle with the world.

The believer can handle the world's temptations and walk before God in victory over the world. It is certain that we must remain a part of the world system until our Lord calls us home to heaven through death or the rapture of the church. Our victory over the world is ours to claim while we live it here and now.

We can have victory through our faith, (1 Jn 5:4-5). "For whatsoever is born of God overcometh the world; and this is the victory that overcometh the world, even our faith. Who is he that overcometh the world, but he that believeth that Jesus is the Son of God" (KJV).

John defines the believer's victory over the world as "our faith." There are two ways in which our faith overcomes the world. In a general sense, our faith includes the whole body of revealed truth which has come to us by the revelation of God. Our faith overcomes the world in this sense by the inner assimilation of God's revealed Word. As

51

the believer becomes grounded in the faith through his understanding of God's Word, all worldy values are measured and overcome by the truth of the Word.

The believer doesn't yield to the world's morality, because through the revealed morality of the Word of God he has a much higher morality. The believer overcomes the worldly provisions of multitudes of false religions because the truth of the Word has grounded him in sound doctrine. The believer doesn't stop preaching the Word when ordered to by the world system because he knows that his faith demands that he preach the Word.

There is a more personal application of the victory of our faith over the world, however, and this comes to us through our union with the Lord Jesus Christ. First John 5:5 states that our overcoming is through believing that Jesus is the Son of God. In John 16:33 the Lord Jesus declared His great victory over the World in these words: "These things I have spoken unto you, that in me ye might have peace. In the world ye shall have tribulation: but be of good cheer; I have overcome the world" (KJV). This verse declares that the hope the disciples have of victory over the tribulations of the world is that Christ has overcome the world. When Jesus Christ died, the doom of the world system and its ruler was settled (Jn 12:31). As by faith believers enter into His victory over the world, they, too, shall overcome and defeat the world. The believer in Christ has victory over the world. This is why it is good to claim the perfect, sinless victorious life Christ lived as a human being on this earth as your daily victory. The world is powerful in its appeal to our flesh. The deceptions of Satan through the world system are very subtle. As we claim our victory in the Lord Jesus Christ, it is His life that secures our victory. He is able to deliver us from this present evil world. He is able to "succor us," or help us right now when the world tempts us (Gal 1:4; Heb 2:18). Because Christ is crucified to the world, so am I (Gal 2:20; 6:14).

What comfort and assurance there is for the believer

who sees how totally our Lord Jesus Christ defeated the world and Satan who rules over the world system. John 16:11 declares, "The prince of this world now stands condemned." As we shall see in more detail in later chapters, this condemnation was accomplished through the victory of the cross. "And having disarmed the powers and authorities, he made a public spectacle of them, triumphing over them by the cross" (Col 2:15). "Since the children have flesh and blood, he too shared in their humanity so that by his death he might destroy him who holds the power of death—that is, the devil—and free those who all their lives were held in slavery by their fear of death" (Heb. 2:14-15).

Our victory is through the One who is in us (Ro 12:2; 1 Jn 4:4). "Ye are of God, little children, and have overcome them: because greater is he that is in you, than he that is in the world" (1 Jn 4:4, KJV).

The inner workings of the Holy Spirit who brings all of the work of the Lord Jesus Christ into our inner being provides part in our victory over the world. He is the One who transforms us by the renewing of our minds. The Holy Spirit brings within us a new appetite and desire that is completely above the world and its enticements. There needs to be a constant reliance upon the Holy Spirit to put within us greater values and desires than those which the world offers. This is why a Spirit-filled Christian finds an inner desire and appetite that enjoys doing things and going places that to a worldling are dull and drab. The inner work of the Holy Spirit has placed within us the fruit of His presence and a newness of life to which the world has no appeal.

Appropriating our victory over the world is a necessary part of our spiritual duty and responsibility. Here is a prayer that is appropriate for claiming one's victory over the world system of things:

Loving heavenly Father, in the name of the Lord Jesus Christ I approach You again in prayer. I glorify You that all of my victory and ability to walk pleasing before You has been provided by Your grace. I desire to claim my victory that You have provided over my enemy, the world system. I recognize its powerful appeal to my fallen fleshly nature. I see that Satan's deception and power in the world is strong against me. I know I cannot overcome the world through my own efforts. I enter into Your provided victory. Thank You that in His humanity, the Lord Jesus Christ overcame the world for me. Thank You that He met all of its temptations for me and defeated them. Thank You that Jesus Christ died and shed His blood that He might accomplish His full victory over the world and its ruler. Thank You that the blood of the Saviour cleanses me of the times I have failed to overcome the world. I enter into my Lord's victory and bring it strong against the appeal of the world to me.

I also open my heart to the full victory of the Holy Spirit over the world. I trust Him to put desires within my being which are above the world. I trust Him to cause the world's appeal to me to be blotted out. May He keep me from being double-minded. I don't want to love the things of God with one part of me and the things of the world with another part of me. May the Holy Spirit unite my heart to fear Your name. May He bring me all together in wholeness to love and serve You with all of my will, my mind, my emotions, my body, and my spirit. Thank You for providing all of my victory. I appropriate it now in the name of the Lord Jesus Christ. Amen.

4

THE SWORD OF THE SPIRIT
IS STILL THE WORD

"Do your best to present yourself to God as one approved, a workman who does not need to be ashamed and who correctly handles the word of truth" (2 Ti 2:15).

THE WORD OF GOD is our only inspired sourcebook on spiritual warfare. Other books are useful only as they are in harmony with the Word of God. It is the Scripture rightly divided and applied that insures our victory. Spiritual warfare should be founded and grounded upon growing use of the Bible. In this chapter will be suggested some approaches to the Bible which should be a continuing part of the warfare of all believers.

First in importance ought to be a program of Scripture memorization and meditation. After sharing with us the importance of claiming our rest and peace in the Lord, Hebrews 4:12 calls our attention to the Word in securing this. "For the word of God is living and active and sharper than any two-edged sword, and piercing as far as the division of soul and spirit, of both joints and marrow, and able to judge the thoughts and intentions of the heart" (NASB).

One cannot help but notice the power of the Word of God to do its workings within us. It brings its life and its active power within us as we let it pierce like the sword. It works in the soul, the spirit, and the body, and ministers to the deeper motivations of our heart.

That's good medicine for all that ails us. No one will become strong in warfare who neglects using the Word of God in an active program of memorization and meditation. The Word of God is God's medicine for all manner of spiritual ills. As you take it in, it does its active work without your awareness of how it is working. If I am ill and the doctor prescribes medication, I take it without understanding all the intricate detail of how it works to help me get well. This is true of the victorious Christian. He is constantly taking in the Word because he knows it is working within him to do all the good things he needs. It is my spiritual nourishment, my spiritual vitamins, my medicine, and my very source of spiritual life.

The best form of memorization would seem to be the committing to memory of larger portions. Memorizing a verse here and there is all right, but it's far better, in most cases, to memorize the verse in its context. To lift a verse out of its context is always somewhat dangerous since it opens the door for a misapplication of God's truth. It is also much easier to memorize whole paragraphs or chapters of the Word because of the natural flow of logic and order in the Word. As I pen these words I am memorizing Romans 8. The flow of the argument of the chapter is beautiful and makes the retention of the chapter much easier. Memorize at your own rate. Keep at it consistently. Use spare moments while driving to work, shaving, washing the dishes, and so on, to be memorizing a portion of the Word of God.

Meditation on the Word is really possible only as you have first committed it to memory. Then no matter where you are or what you are doing, if your mind is free to think, you can begin to meditate on a passage word by word, line by line, and verse by verse. Complete new insights will come to you as you let the Holy Spirit open the text to your understanding. Memorization and meditation upon the Word of God is perhaps the single greatest step a believer can take in helping him overcome the world, the flesh, and the devil.

The Word of God needs also to be systematically read and studied as it relates to our enemies. Biblical insight into how Satan operates, where he came from, and who he is provides strong equipment in spiritual warfare. The believer intent on claiming all of his victory in the Lord Jesus Christ should familiarize himself with basic biblical information about his enemy. The remainder of this chapter will be given to extensive Bible quotations about Satan.

I. Satan's Original State (Eze 28:12-17). This passage on the Tyrian king symbolizes Satan and provides us with insight into Satan's state as created by God.
A. He was created full of wisdom and beauty (v. 12). "Thus says the Lord GOD, You had the seal of perfection, Full of wisdom and perfect in beauty" (NASB).
B. He was given a place on God's holy mountain (v. 14). "You were on the holy mountain of God; You walked in the midst of the stones of fire" (NASB).
C. He was created a holy and righteous being (v. 15). "You were blameless in your ways From the day you were created" (NASB).
D. Pride in his heart was the beginning of his fall (v. 17). "Your heart was lifted up because of your beauty; You corrupted your wisdom by reason of your splendor. I cast you to the ground" (NASB).

II. Satan's Rebellion and Fall (Is 14:12-15).
A. Lucifer sought to exalt himself to the position of Jehovah (vv. 13-14). "But you said in your heart, 'I will ascend to heaven; I will raise my throne above the stars of God. And I will sit on the mount of assembly In the recesses of the north. I will ascend above the heights of the clouds; I will make myself like the Most High'" (NASB).

57

B. In his vanity he declared, "I will be like God." It was this act of his will in rebellion that caused him to fall and become the devil and Satan.

III. Satan's Titles and Names.
A. His many names describe his activity, showing him to be a devious enemy.
1. *Satan* means "adversary" (Zec 3:1; 1 Pe 5:8). He is a constant relentless opponent. "Be self-controlled and alert. Your enemy the devil prowls around like a roaring lion looking for someone to devour" (1 Pe 5:8).
2. He is the accuser. "Then I heard a loud voice in heaven say: 'Now have come the salvation and the power and the kingdom of our God, and the authority of his Christ. For the accuser of our brothers, who accuses them before our God day and night, has been hurled down'" (Rev 12:10). Satan's desire is to cause us to condemn ourselves. He wants to cause a believer to have a vagueness about what he has done wrong and seeks to keep him from knowing what to do about his sin. This is opposite to the conviction of the Holy Spirit. The Holy Spirit convicts us of definite sins and shows us that through the shed blood of Christ there is cleansing and forgiveness.
3. *Lucifer* means "light bearer" (Is 14:12). In his fallen state, Satan comes as an angel of light to deceive the very elect.
4. He is called the dragon. This pictures the baseness and fierceness of this enemy. "And there was war in heaven. Michael and his angels fought against the dragon, and the dragon and his angels fought back" (Rev 12:7).
5. *Devil* means "slanderer" (1 Pe 5:8). Satan likes nothing better than to defame and slander God's own before others.
6. He is called a murderer and a liar. "You belong to your father, the devil, and you want to carry out your

father's desire. He was a murderer from the beginning, not holding to the truth, for there is no truth in him. When he lies, he speaks his native language, for he is a liar and the father of lies" (Jn 8:44). Satan wants to murder believers and seeks to deceive us by lies.

7. He is the deceiver. "And the devil, who deceived them, was thrown into the lake of burning sulfur" (Rev 20:10). In all ways he can, Satan wants to lead us to believe that which is not true.

8. Satan is the prince of this world. "Now is the time for judgement on this world; now the prince of this world will be driven out" (Jn 12:31). Satan operates as a powerful manipulator in the affairs of the world.

9. He is the prince of the power of the air. "You followed the ways of this world and of the ruler [prince] of the kingdom of the air, the spirit who is now at work in those who are disobedient" (Ephesians 2:2). This would indicate that Satan's realm of movement is in the atmosphere surrounding the earth. Christ ascended through Satan's very realm to display openly His victory.

10. He is called the destroyer. The Greek and Hebrew words in Revelation 9:11 mean destroyer. "They had as king over them the angel of the Abyss, whose name in Hebrew is Abaddon, and in Greek, Apollyon." Satan attempts to destroy all that is holy and precious to God.

11. He is the tempter. "The tempter came to him and said, 'If you are the Son of God, tell these stones to become bread'" (Mt 4:3).

12. Satan is the evil one. "The weeds are the sons of the evil one" (Mt 13:38).

13. He is the god of this age. "The god of this age has blinded the minds of unbelievers, so that they cannot see the light of the gospel of the glory of Christ, who is the image of God" (2 Co 4:4).

IV. Satan's Awesome Power.
  A. Not even a saved believer can ignore Satan's power
     to defeat him apart from God's provided victory.
     "Put on the full armor of God so that you can take
     your stand against the devil's schemes. For our
     struggle is not against flesh and blood, but against
     the rulers, against the authorities, against the powers
     of this dark world and against the spiritual forces of
     evil in the heavenly realms" (Eph 6:11-12).

  B. He is the absolute sovereign over the realm of de-
     mons. "Jesus was driving out a demon that was
     mute. When the demon left, the man who had been
     dumb spoke, and the crowd was amazed. But some of
     them said, 'By Beelzebub, the prince of demons, he is
     driving out demons.' Others tested him by asking for
     a sign from heaven. Jesus knew their thoughts and
     said to them, 'Any kingdom divided against itself
     will be ruined, and a house divided against itself will
     fall. If Satan is divided against himself, how can his
     kingdom stand?" (Lk 11:14-18).
  1. He has a throne. "I know where you live—where
     Satan has his throne" (Rev 2:13).
  2. He rules a kingdom. "If Satan drives out Satan, he is
     divided against himself. How then can his kingdom
     stand?" (Mt 12:26).
  3. He subtly masquerades as an angel of light. "And no
     wonder, for Satan himself masquerades as an angel
     of light. It is not surprising, then, if his servants
     masquerade as servants of righteousness. Their end
     will be what their actions deserve" (2 Co 11:14-15).
  4. He has meeting places. "I know the slander of those
     who say they are Jews and are not, but are a
     synagogue of Satan" (Rev 2:9).

  C. He has power to oppose the mightiest of angels. "But
     even the archangel Michael, when he was disputing
     the devil about the body of Moses, did not dare to
     bring a slanderous accusation against him, but said,

'The Lord rebuke you!' " (Jude 9; see also Dan 10:5, 12-13).

D. He maneuvers and holds in bondage the realm of lost man. "We know that we are the children of God, and that the whole world is under the control of the evil one" (1 Jn 5:19).

E. Satan's power is limited only by the will of almighty God. " 'Hast Thou not made a hedge about him and his house and all that he has, on every side? Thou hast blessed the work of his hands, and his possessions have increased in the land. But put forth Thy hand now and touch all that he has; he will surely curse Thee to Thy face.' Then the LORD said to Satan, 'Behold, all that he has is in your power, only do not put forth your hand on him.' So Satan departed from the presence of the LORD" (Job 1:10-12, NASB).

V. Satan's Sphere of Activity.

A. He still has permitted access to heaven. "Now there was a day when the sons of God came to present themselves before the LORD, Satan also came among them" (Job 1:6, NASB; see also Rev 12:7-10).

B. His particular field of operation is the earth. "And the LORD said to Satan, 'From where do you come?' Then Satan answered the LORD and said, 'From roaming about the earth and walking around on it.' " (Job 1:7, NASB; see also 1 Pe 5:8).

VI. Satan's Strategy of Work.

A. He authored sin and continues to agitate man to sin. "Now the serpent was more crafty than any beast of the field which the LORD God had made. And he said to the woman, 'Indeed, and has God said "You shall not eat from any tree of the garden"?' And the woman said to the serpent, 'From the fruit of the trees of the garden we may eat; but from the fruit of the tree which is in the middle,... God has said, "You shall not eat from it or touch it, lest you die." ' And the serpent said,...'You surely shall not die! For God knows that in the day you eat from it your eyes will be opened, and you will be like God, knowing good and evil.' When the woman saw that the tree was good for food and that it was a delight to the eyes, and that the tree was desirable to make one wise, she took from its fruit and ate; and she gave also to her husband with her, and he ate" (Gen 3:1-6, NASB).

B. He causes sickness and suffering. "God anointed Jesus of Nazareth with the Holy Spirit and power, and how he went around doing good and healing all who were under the power of the devil, because God was with him" (Ac 10:38).

C. He has the power of death. "Since the children have flesh and blood, he too shared in their humanity so that by his death he might destroy him who holds the power of death—that is, the devil" (Heb 2:14).

D. He provides snares or traps for men. "He must also have a good reputation with outsiders, so that he will not fall into disgrace and into the devil's trap" (1 Ti 3:7).

E. He injects wicked purposes into man's heart. "The evening meal was being served, and the devil had already prompted Judas Iscariot, son of Simon, to betray Jesus" (Jn 13:2; see also Ac 5:3).

F. He can personally enter and control a man. "As soon as Judas took the bread, Satan entered into him" (Jn 13:27).

G. He seeks to take away the Word of God from our understanding. "As soon as they hear it, Satan comes and takes away the word that was sown in them" (Mk 4:15).

H. He places the false among God's own. "The enemy who sows them is the devil" (Mt 13:39).

I. He attempts to torment God's servants. "Simon, Simon, Satan has asked to sift you all as wheat" (Lk 22:31; see also 2 Co 12:7).

J. He can hinder God's servants from carrying out their desires. "For we wanted to come to you—certainly I,

Paul, did, again and again—but Satan stopped us" (1 Th 2:18).

K. He casts God's servants into prison. "I tell you, the devil will put some of you in prison to test you, and you will suffer persecution for ten days. Be faithful, even to the point of death, and I will give you the crown of life" (Rev 2:10).

L. He accuses believers before Christ. "Now have come the salvation and the power and the kingdom of our God, and the authority of his Christ. For the accuser of our brothers, who accuses them before our God day and night, has been hurled down" (Rev 12:10).

VII. Satan's Destiny.

A. He is under the sentence of doom. "Nevertheless you will be thrust down to Sheol, to the recesses of the pit" (Is 14:15, NASB).

B. He is under an unending curse. "And the LORD God said to the serpent, 'Because you have done this, Cursed are you more than all cattle, And more than every beast of the field; on your belly shall you go, and dust shall you eat All the days of your life; And I will put enmity Between you and the woman, And between your seed and her seed; He shall bruise you on the head, And you shall bruise him on the heel" (Gen 3:14-15, NASB).

C. He will be cast out of heaven during the tribulation. "And there was war in heaven. Michael and his angels fought against the dragon, and the dragon and his angels fought back. But he was not strong enough, and they lost their place in heaven. The great dragon was hurled down—that ancient serpent called the devil or Satan, who leads the world astray. He was hurled to the earth, and his angels with him" (Rev 12:7-10).

D. During the earthly reign of Christ, Satan will be bound in the bottomless pit. "And I saw an angel coming down out of heaven, having the key to the

Abyss and holding in his hand a great chain. He seized the dragon, that ancient serpent, who is the devil, or Satan, and bound him for a thousand years. He threw him into the Abyss, and locked and sealed it over him, to keep him from deceiving the nations any more until the thousand years were ended. After that, he must be set free for a short time" (Rev 20:1-3).
E. Satan will be eternally consigned to the lake of fire. "And the devil, who deceived them, was thrown into the lake of burning sulfur, where the beast and the false prophet had been thrown. They will be tormented day and night for ever and ever" (Rev 20:10).

VIII. The Believer's Victory over Satan.
  A. The triumph of Jesus Christ is the surety of the believer's victory (Mt 4:1-11; Ro 5:12-19).
  1. Christ defeated Satan at the cross and has given that victory to all believers. "He who does what is sinful is of the devil, because the devil has been sinning from the beginning. The reason the Son of God appeared was to destroy the devil's work" (1 Jn 3:8; see also Col 2:15; Heb 2:14-15).

  2. In our Lord's exaltation, the believer has the Saviour's victory imputed to him. "That power is like the working of his mighty strength, which he exerted in Christ when he raised him from the dead and seated him at his right hand in the heavenly realms, far above all rule and authority, power and dominion, and every title that can be given, not only in the present age but also in the one to come. And God placed all things under his feet and appointed him to be head over everything for the church, which is his body, the fullness of him who fills everything in every way" (Eph 1:19-23). "God, who is rich in mercy, made us alive with Christ even when we were dead in transgressions—it is by grace you have been saved. And God raised us up with Christ and seated

us with him in heavenly realms in Christ Jesus" (Eph 2:4-6; see also Heb 1:13; 1 Pe 3:22).

B. Through God's salvation, the believer is legally set free from Satan's power. "To open their eyes and turn them from darkness to light, and from the power of Satan to God so that they may receive forgiveness of sins and a place among those who are sanctified by faith in me." (Ac 26:18; see also Lk 10:17-20; 2 Co 4:4; Eph 2:1-3; Col 1:13).

C. Through his sanctified walk with God, the believer maintains his legally purchased freedom.

1. He must yield to God and resist the devil. "Submit yourselves, then, to God. Resist the devil, and he will flee from you" (Ja 4:7; see also 1 Pe 5:8).

2. He must not give ground or foothold to Satan through fleshly sin. "And do not give the devil a foothold" (Eph 4:27).

3. He must put on his provided protection in the whole armor of God. "Finally, be strong in the Lord and in his mighty power. Put on the full armor of God so that you can take your stand against the devil's schemes. For our struggle is not against flesh and blood, but against the rulers, against the authorities, against the powers of this dark world and against the spiritual forces of evil in the heavenly realms. Therefore put on the full armor of God, so that when the day of evil comes, you may be able to stand your ground, and after you have done everything, to stand. Stand firm then, with the belt of truth buckled around your waist, with the breastplate of righteousness in place, and with your feet fitted with the gospel of peace as a firm footing. In addition to all this, take up the shield of faith, with which you can extinguish all the flaming arrows of the evil one. Take the helmet of salvation and the sword of the Spirit, which is the Word of God. And pray in the Spirit on all occasions with all kinds of prayers and

requests. With this in mind, be alert and always keep on praying for all the saints" (Eph 6:10-18).

4. There are special warnings for us to heed against Satan's tactics. The suggested portions of Scripture listed below although not quoted are worthy of careful investigation on the part of any believer who desires a victorious walk and the defeat of Satan in his life.

  a. Do not accuse others judgmentally (2 Co 2:1-11).
  b. Avoid hypocritical actions (Ac 5:1-11).
  c. Do not disobey what is known to be God's will (Eph 4:17-32).
  d. Make sure that your testimony is consistently obvious to all men (1 Ti 3:7).
  e. Constantly guard against pride (1 Ti 3:6).
  f. Avoid a striving, contentious spirit (2 Ti 2:23-26).

It is vital for the believer to be sure of his ground and his certain victory through the Lord Jesus Christ in combatting the forces of darkness. It is not unusual to be challenged by a wicked spirit who contests your authority when commanding him to depart to the place the Lord Jesus Christ sends him. The quoting of the Word and pressing it constantly against the contesting spirit always brings victory. The Word cannot be broken.

5

FACING SATAN'S KINGDOM

"Put on the whole armour of God, that ye may be able to stand against the wiles of the devil" (Eph 6:11, KJV).

Hundreds Stand In Line to See Exorcist. Psychiatrist Warns of Danger in Seeing Exorcist. Never in my memory has any film received such headline coverage in the newspapers as *The Exorcist* is receiving. This sensationalized, fear-producing film about Satan and demon possession has hit America with stunning emotional impact.

"Pastor, you've got to say something from the pulpit about this film, *The Exorcist.* Everybody is talking about it, and many are going to see it out of curiosity. People with whom I work are really torn up after they've seen it."

"Pastor, can we have a seminar for our children and young people on the dangers of getting involved in all of this occultism? My children are really confused. All the kids at school are talking about their new experimentation with the spirit world. I believe we've got to inform our children about what the Bible says about such things."

"Have you seen the flood of television commercials advertising this new magazine on witchcraft? Can't we do something as a church to stop this open promotion of Satan's program?"

People are talking and deeply concerned about this new interest in the world of the occult. Interest has spread through our culture like an epidemic. Grandmothers and youngsters alike browse over the occult literature at the local drugstore. This abounding interest in Satan's realm is making its impact felt upon the Christian community as well as the world system.

Satan and the kingdom of darkness over which he rules pose a constant challenge and threat to the effectiveness and stability of believers. It is my conviction that if our Lord were to remove from us His protection and shielding for even a moment, Satan would not hesitate to kill us. He did not get his title of murderer without good cause. In Job's trials, the Lord specifically restrained Satan from taking Job's life, indicating that this righteous servant would have been killed had the Lord not restrained Satan.

As believers consider their warfare against Satan, two extremes must be carefully avoided. The first extreme is the tendency to ignore this enemy and to treat the whole subject of demonology lightly. One of Satan's clever strategies against us is to keep us in ignorance of his power and working. A pastor friend once stated to me his conviction that if he would just occupy himself with the gospel, the winning of souls, and the Person of the Lord Jesus Christ, he would not have to be too concerned about Satan. Such a view sounds very pious and spiritual, but it is very unbiblical and dangerous. Any believer who determines to occupy himself with the gospel, the winning of the lost, and knowing the Lord Jesus Christ is going to be a special target of Satan. To ignore the weapons of our warfare provided by the Lord against Satan and his kingdom is spiritual suicide. We will soon meet spiritual disaster if we ignore this enemy.

The other extreme to be avoided is a fearful preoccupation with Satan and his kingdom. It is a strategy of Satan to make us more conscious and aware of Satan and his kingdom than we are of the heavenly Father, the Lord Jesus Christ, and the blessed Holy Spirit. The great emphasis of the Word of God is upon the accomplished victory which is ours to appropriate and claim through our Lord Jesus Christ. Though recognizing the awesome power and cunning of Satan, the entire tenor of Scripture affirms that Satan is a defeated foe. One of the tragedies of the film and literature previously mentioned is its exalting of the power of Satan.

It is a common problem of those under the attack of Satan to become preoccupied with thoughts about how Satan is tempting, afflicting, or oppressing them rather than meditating on the victory Christ has won. To be aware of this danger is a helpful step toward the avoidance of too much occupation with thought about Satan. Dr. A. W. Tozer has brought this danger of too much occupation with Satan into perspective with his inimitable style and depth:

> The scriptural way to see things is to set the Lord always before us, put Christ in the center of our vision, and if Satan is lurking around he will appear on the margin only and be seen as but a shadow on the edge of the brightness. It is always wrong to reverse this — to set Satan in the focus of our vision and push God out to the margin. Nothing but tragedy can come of such inversion.
>
> The best way to keep the enemy out is to keep Christ in. The sheep need not be terrified by the wolf; they have but to stay close to the shepherd. It is not the praying sheep Satan fears, but the presence of the shepherd.
>
> The instructed Christian whose faculties have been developed by the Word and the Spirit will not fear the devil. When necessary he will stand against the powers of darkness and overcome them by the blood of the Lamb and the word of his testimony. He will recognize the peril in which he lives and will know what to do about it, but he will practice the presence of God and never allow himself to become devil-conscious.*

Satan is a personal spirit being who is just as real and living as you or I. He controls a vast and highly structured

*A. W. Tozer, *Born After Midnight* (Harrisburg: Christian Pubns., 1959) p. 43.

kingdom of personal spirit beings who have the same wicked intent and purpose as Satan in opposing God's will and plans.

This vast kingdom of darkness is centering its strategy against mankind. There are some deep and obvious theological reasons why this is so. It is not our purpose to go into these reasons here, but rather to proceed to understand our resources against this attack. Beginning with Satan's subtle attack against Adam and Eve, and on throughout the Bible, those who are in vital communion and fellowship with God are the very ones who must face this enemy in his most devious strategy.

The apostle Paul seems to have experienced in his lifetime a growing and enlarging understanding of his own spiritual battles with the devil. His epistles contain numerous references to this great battle, but the epistle to the Ephesians is the Christian's handbook on spiritual warfare against the devil and his kingdom. The awesomeness of the battle and the surety of our victory both are spelled out for us in Ephesians 6:10-18. Consider with me some important principles for effective warfare against Satan to be gleaned from this classic text.

First, it is the will of God for all believers that we be "strong in the Lord and the power of his might" (Ephesians 6:10, KJV). There is no reason for the believer to be defeated and destroyed by Satan's power. We are to remain strong and powerful foes of all that Satan purposes to do. His most sophisticated strategy and concentrated power need not be a threat to any believer. Strength in the Lord, all the mighty power we need, is available. What an important fact that is. Warfare against Satan must be approached from this perspective. As we avail ourselves of our resources, we'll still be standing when the smoke clears away from the battlefield and the enemy will be in retreat and ultimately trampled under our feet (Ro 16:20).

Another important principle of warfare against Satan is to have a biblical understanding of what we are up against. Paul tells us in Ephesians 6:10 that we must put on the whole armor of God that we might stand against the wiles of the devil. That word *wiles* conveys the picture of a cunning, crafty, sneaky enemy. He is extremely subtle and clever about the way he works against us. How very true this is. With Christians he delights to play both ends against the middle. As the tempter, he delights to inject into our minds wicked thoughts and desires. Then as the accuser, he loves to taunt us about what a terrible person we are to ever have such wicked and sinful thoughts as those. We must expect that Satan will use the most devious, sneaky, and subtle strategy against us which can only be seen and determined as the Lord illumines His Word and bestows His wisdom upon us.

This understanding of our foe also entails an awareness of the powers of darkness that work with him in his kingdom of darkness. Ephesians 6:12 provides us with one of the clearest pictures of this kingdom you will find anyplace in the Word. Our warfare is not a battle with flesh and blood enemies. How much easier it would be if that were so. If you could only see these foes and know when they are near like you can see another human being! But Satan's kingdom is one of spirit beings you cannot see or handle. Mystery writers have often developed the theme of the advantage the invisible man would have over common mortals. These beings are spirit beings, nonmaterial and invisible, but no less real. We will wrestle with them. This means hand-to-hand combat. When I was in high school, I was on the wrestling team for a time. Wrestling is one of the most fatiguing of all competitive sports. The pitting of skill and muscle against one's opponent in such sport is extremely demanding.

This is the kind of battle we face with these invisible spirit beings. The picture is one of close, demanding, fatiguing encounter.

These spirit beings are also very structured, organized and disciplined. We gain insight into this fact by the mention of these foes who serve under Satan's control in Ephesians 6:12. The picture is one much like that which

71

prevails in a military organization. At the top of America's military structure is our President, the commander-in-chief of all military forces. Under him are the commanding generals, the admirals, and all of the other officers on down to the lowly private.

This is the same kind of structure which is suggested here in Ephesians 6. Satan is the commander-in-chief of the forces of darkness. He is the supreme strategist, and under him is a highly organized system which is as disciplined to carry out Satan's wishes as he can make it.

The first level under Satan is a group of commanders called *principalities* or *princes*. These powerful beings carry vast responsibility and power to guide the affairs of Satan. I believe there are different levels of authority among these princes. We gain insight into their working and power in the Old Testament incident recorded in Daniel 10 between the angelic messenger from God sent to speak to Daniel and the prince of Persia (Dan. 10:13). When the angelic messenger finally arrived after a three-week delay, he explained that his delay was because of the prince of Persia's resistance. Only after Michael the archangel came to do battle against this prince was the special angelic messenger able to complete his journey to Daniel. Does this not suggest that Satan has a prince over every nation whose responsibility it is to carry out Satan's diabolical plans against that nation? Under him are other princes who guide the plans of Satan against the political structure, or the educational structure, or the entertainment structure of that nation.

The next level down in this organized structure are the *powers*. These are probably more numerous and somewhat less independent and powerful than the princes. Yet their name suggests very powerful activity which they are capable of addressing against believers.

The next level down in the organization of evil are the *rulers of darkness.* These beings are more numerous; yet they are the real workhorses on the command level. Their counterpart in the army might be the lieutenants and sergeants of our military forces. These rulers of darkness have directly under them a very vast final level of spirit beings called *spiritual wickedness* or *wicked spirits* in high places. I understand these to be the demons so often mentioned during the earthly life of our Lord. These beings are multitudinous, so much so that a whole legion dwelt in one lone man, according to Mark 5:9.

These are the personal wicked spirit forces which we must battle. Formidable indeed is the picture the Word presents to us of this crafty, invisible, highly organized, wicked system of evil with which by the very nature of the case we must battle. We have no choice; the enemy presses the battle to us, and it is God's sovereign will and purpose in this day that we fight a good fight.

The third general principle of our warfare against Satan seen in Ephesians 6:10-18 is the importance of the provided armor of God. As believers we are to aggressively act in taking the armor and putting it on. Some have questioned what this armor is and when or how often should we put it on.

The answer to how often seems fairly obvious. Every time we face the enemy and battle him we should be sure our armor is in place. Daily we need to appropriate our provided armor and put on our spiritual dress for battle. To me, this text indicates the battle will be there on a daily basis. A very close, hard-fought battle is always before us. Facing that battle without armor is unthinkable.

Putting on the armor has a further purpose and benefit which must not be missed. I came upon this as a result of personal experience. As a result of my own desire to put on the armor for battle on a daily basis, I began to seek to understand each part of the armor and to discover what the Bible has to say about these various parts of our spiritual dress. Putting on the armor is something done by prayer and the daily practice of faith. As you equip yourself with the whole armor of God, you will find yourself meditating on the armor and using it many times throughout the day. It is a very worshipful and praising experience to meditate upon each piece of the armor provided for us by God. This is the *whole* armor of God. It is a complete, total provision of God, sufficient to equip us to stand against the very worst Satan can dish out. Following is a typical prayer one might use in putting on his armor, seeking to show how it can enlarge into a worship and praise experience of adoration of our Lord.

Heavenly Father, I desire to be obedient by being strong in the Lord and the power of Your might. I see that this is Your will and purpose for me. I recognize that it is essential to put on the armor that You have provided, and I do so now with gratitude and praise that You have provided all I need to stand in victory against Satan and his kingdom. Grant me wisdom to discern the tactics and sneakiness of Satan's strategy against me. Enable me to wrestle in victory against the princes, powers, rulers, and wicked spirits who carry the battle of darkness against me.

I delight to take the armor You have provided and by faith to put it on as effective spiritual protection against the spiritual forces of darkness.

I confidently take the loin girdle of truth that You offer me. I take Him who is the truth as my strength and protection. I reject Satan's lies and deceiving ways to gain advantage against me. Grant me discernment and wisdom to recognize the subtle deceiving ways in which Satan seeks to cause me to accept his lies as truth. I desire to believe only the truth, to live the truth, to speak the truth, and to know the truth. I worship and praise You that You lead me only in the ways of truth. Thank You that Satan cannot stand against the bold use of truth.

Thank You for the breastplate of righteousness which you offer me. I eagerly accept it and put it on as my protection.

Thank You for reminding me again that all of my righteousness comes from You. I embrace that righteousness which is mine by faith in the Lord Jesus Christ. It is His righteousness that is mine through justification. I reject and repudiate all trust in my own righteousness which is as filthy rags. I ask You to cleanse me of all the times I have counted my own goodness as being acceptable before You. I bring the righteousness of my Lord directly against all of Satan's workings against me. I express my desire to walk in righteousness before God today. By faith I appropriate the righteousness of Christ and invite Him to walk in His holiness in my life today that I might experience His righteousness in total context of ordinary living. I count upon the righteousness of my Lord to be my protection. I know that Satan must retreat from before the righteousness of God.

Thank You, Lord, for the sandals of peace You have provided. I desire that my feet should stand on the solid rock of the peace that You have provided. I claim the peace with God which is mine through justification. I desire the peace of God which touches my emotions and feelings through prayer and sanctification (Phil 4:6). Thank You that as I walk in obedience to You that the God of peace promises to walk with me (Phil 4:9), that as the God of peace You are putting Satan under my feet (Ro 16:20). I will share this good news of peace with all others today that Your Spirit will bring into my life and witness. Thank You that You have not given me the spirit of fear but of love and power and a sound mind (2 Ti 1:7). Thank You that Satan cannot stand against Your peace.

Eagerly, Lord, I lift up the shield of faith against all the blazing missiles that Satan and his hosts fire at me. I recognize that You are my shield and that in Your incarnation and crucifixion You took the arrows of Satan which I deserved. By faith I count upon You to shield me from above and beneath; on my right and my left; in front of me and behind me, that I might be protected, walled in, encapsulated by You that Satan may gain no way to hurt or destroy me from fulfilling Your will today. I am willing that any fiery darts of Satan You wish to touch me should do so, but I shall look upon them as refining fires permitted in Your providence for my refining and glory (1 Pe 1).

Thank You, Lord, that You are a complete and perfect shield and that Satan cannot touch me apart from Your sovereign purpose.

I recognize that my mind is a particular target of Satan's deceiving ways. I take from You the helmet of salvation. I cover my mind, my thoughts, with Your salvation. I recognize that the Lord Jesus Christ is my salvation. I helmet my head with Him. I invite His mind to be in me. Let me think His thoughts, feel His love and compassion, and discern His will and leading in all things. Let my mind be occupied with the continuing, daily, saving work of my Lord in and through my life. May the salvation of my Lord meet and defeat all Satanic thoughts that come to my mind.

With joy I take hold upon the sword of the Spirit, which is the Word of God. I affirm that Your Word is the trustworthy, infallible Word of God. I choose to believe it and to live in its truth and power. Grant me the love for Your Word which comes from the Holy Spirit. Forgive and cleanse me from the sin of neglecting Your Word. Enable me to memorize it and to meditate upon its truth. Grant me proficient recall and skill in using Your Word against all of Satan's subtle attacks against me, even as my Lord Jesus Christ used the Word against Satan. Enable me to use Your Word not only to defend me from Satan, but also to claim its promises and to wield the sword strong against Satan to defeat him, to push him back, to take away from him ground he claims, and to win great victories for my God through Your Word. Thank You that Satan must retreat from Your Word applied against him.

Thank You, dear Lord, for prayer. Help me to keep this armor well oiled with prayer. I desire to pray at all times with depth and intensity as the Holy Spirit leads me. I reject all fleshly praying as sin. I trust the Holy Spirit to enable me, to intercede for me and through me. Grant me great supplication and burden for others in God's family of blood-washed saints. Enable me to see their needs and to assist them through prayer as the enemy attacks them. All of these petitions, intercessions, and words of praise I *offer up before the true and living God in the name and worthy merit of my Lord Jesus Christ. Amen.*

Putting on one's armor in prayer may be shortened or greatly extended even beyond the prayer suggested. The important thing is to put on your armor. See its vital importance and appropriate what our Lord offers to you for your victory and protection. How tragic and heartbreaking it is to see believers reeling and staggering under Satan's assault with little hope of victory. The victory is already provided. It remains for us only to aggressively use it and not passively assume it.

6

UNDERSTAND AND DON'T BE AFRAID

"For God hath not given us the spirit of fear; but of power, and of love, and of a sound mind" (2 Ti 1:7, KJV).

"CLAIMING MY FULL AUTHORITY over you through my union with the Lord Jesus Christ, I command you to reveal how you were able to gain control in this person's life. I hold the blood of Christ against you and command you to tell me."

"She is afraid. We made her afraid. She's full of fear."

"Is that the ground you claim against this child of God? Are you able to torment and work this destruction in her life because of fear?"

"Yes, she is afraid all the time, and we can work through her fear."

This conversation is reproduced as nearly as I can recall it from my memory and from notes taken during an aggressive confrontation against the powers of darkness troubling a believer's life. Through her faculties, the response from these spiritual enemies was very definite and strong. By claiming the victory of our Lord Jesus Christ, she was delivered from the plague of their persistent activity.

Fearfulness is not of God. The Holy Spirit is not one who makes us fearful; rather He gives us spiritual power, a heart full of love, and a mind that is sound and understanding.

Fear comes from another spirit. Satan and his demons are quick to author fear. The apostle Peter calls us to: "Be sober, be vigilant; because your adversary the devil, as a roaring lion, walketh about seeking whom he may devour: whom resist stedfast in the faith" (1 Pe 5:8-9a, KJV).

The roaring of the king of beasts is an awesome and fear-producing sound, particularly if you happen to be the target for devouring. An old lion will often get on one side of the prey and roar vociferously, producing fear in the prey and causing it to run toward the younger lions waiting in ambush to leap out and kill the victim. Satan roars that he might make us afraid. Fear is the opposite of faith. Fear gives Satan an unusual advantage over us. Fear numbs and dulls our alertness and has the capacity to make us freeze in terror. The roar of a lion can actually paralyze some prey he stalks, causing the victim to be an early target for destruction. The same is true of believers who are the target for Satan's devouring. If he can create fear in us, we are much easier prey for him to destroy. Christians greatly err when they avoid the subject of spiritual warfare because of the fearsome power of Satan.

It has been my experience to hear what I consider to be a very tragic statement concerning warfare with Satan. There are those who say that if you are not aware of any particular attack of Satan upon you, it is best to avoid any active study of Satan and his working because many who do make such a study come under particular harassment from Satan and his kingdom. It deeply concerns me to hear such a statement, because it appears to be built upon the principle of fear.

According to such thought, Satan is so fearsome and powerful that we'd best not challenge him because of the personal cost to us.

Satan is an enemy to be respected and understood for his God-created and granted position and power, but we must not fear him. To do so is to fail to appreciate the Person and work of our Lord Jesus Christ. The victory of Christ over Satan is total and complete. The person who appropriates and applies by faith the victory which Christ has purchased and provided will find a gracious, God-authored courage stabilizing his inner man.

It is a very human and natural response of man to fear the unknown. For a believer to keep himself in the dark about Satan's person and work is a dangerous mistake. If this enemy with whom we personally have so much to do in battle remains to us some mysterious, foreboding awesome power we are afraid to oppose, we are indeed at a disadvantage. From a biblical perspective, we should know all we can about Satan's tactics and his methods of attack against us. We must also know the biblical basis of our victory over Satan and his world of darkness.

Just as there are definite ways in which the flesh tempts us to sin, and the world seeks to force us into its mold, so there are ways in which Satan tempts us to rebel and miss the will of God for our lives.

Satan seeks to coordinate these three powerful enemies against us into a form of attack that will defeat and utterly destroy our conformity to the will of God. Going beyond that, he even tries to make us pawns to carry forth Satan's will and plans. Second Corinthians 2:11 reminds us that we need not be ignorant of Satan's devices.

Consider some of the more obvious strategies of attack Satan devises against us. The Word calls him the adversary. (Zec 3:1; 1 Pe 5:8). This means that he is a contentious opponent who keeps needling us in relentless opposition.

One of his most subtle methods of attack is to cause us to act independently of God and to act upon decisions that are contrary to the will of God. This is evident in his first temptation to man in the garden. In Genesis 3 the genius of the temptation to Eve was that she would be as wise as God and independent from God if she'd eat of the forbidden fruit. In that temptation he cast doubt upon God's Word: "Did God really say?" He questioned God's goodness: "Is God trying to keep back from you something that's good for you?" He questioned God's truthfulness: "You'll not die;" he declared. "God lied to you." He questioned God's motive: "God doesn't want you to be as wise as He is." He sought to exalt man's wisdom to God's level: "You'll be as wise as God."

Satan will always be around to lead us to act independent of God in times of decision. He will do all he can to deceive us into acting in any matter independent of God's leading or expressed will in the Word. All times of decision in a person's life are of major importance. Such times must be bathed in prayer. Decisions should be made without compromise of biblical principle and should show confidence in the Holy Spirit's leading.

Further, Satan tempts us to lie or to believe his lie. In John 8:44 the Lord Jesus Christ calls Satan a liar and the father of it. He will constantly tempt a believer to lie or to believe the lie. Ananias and Sapphira fell for this work of Satan against them. "Satan . . . filled your heart that you have lied to the Holy Spirit" (Ac 5:3).

Satan and his demons are terrible liars. Everything they say and do has the lie as its foundation. Even when he speaks the truth, his motivation is to lie and deceive. In his temptations to the Lord Jesus in the wilderness, he quoted the truth of the Word, but his false application was a deception and a lie. No wonder in the context of warfare against Satan and in the context of the warning to not give place to the devil, the apostle Paul writes, "Wherefore putting away lying, speak every man truth with his neighbour" (Eph 4:25, KJV). Lying is peculiarly a Satanic temptation to sin against God and man.

In his role as the accuser, Satan tempts us (Rev 12:10). He is a relentless opponent in this endeavor to bring us under false guilt and self-condemnation. He delights to play both ends against the middle. If he can get this working for him, he will very nearly live up to his reputation as the destroyer. He likes nothing better than to project into the mind of a believer vile, evil thoughts and desires, and then to taunt his accusations. "What kind of a Christian are you to have such wicked thoughts as those?" This is one of his most effective and common methods of attack against sincere believers. How believers need to be careful in this matter of accusing or judging other Christians! To fall into this trap is to peculiarly align oneself with the work of Satan as the accuser of the brethren.

Satan battles us through hard circumstances and physical assault, and attempts to kill us. John 8:44 calls Satan a murderer. In Job's experience with Satan's temptations, the focus of attack was upon his physical person and all that he had. This enemy would rob us of all we have and then murder us if God did not restrain him.

Satan tempts us not to forgive others (2 Co 2:10-11). An unforgiving spirit is particularly satanic and gives Satan an advantage over us. Many sincere believers fall into this snare of Satan.

Satan tempts us to be filled with pride and vainglory (1 Ti 3:6). To be lifted up with pride is to fall under the condemnation of the devil. Exalting self, seeking praise and credit for our own human ability, is a very telling temptation of Satan.

Satan's purpose in getting us to yield to his temptation is always that he might bring us more deeply under his control and dominion. There are some very sobering statements in the Word about what hold Satan can place upon Christians. We must take seriously such Scripture warnings as the danger of Satan gaining an advantage over us (2 Co 2:10-11), or the sobering possibility of falling into the condemnation of the devil (1 Ti 3:6), and the bondage threat of falling into the snare of the devil and being taken captive by him at his will (2 Ti 2:26).

This raises the question for us of how subject a Christian is to Satan's control and domination. There remains the disturbing question as to whether or not a Christian can be actually demon possessed. Let's look at this question from a biblical perspective.

I know of no more fear-producing thought to many believers than the slightest hint that a Christian might be possessed by some of Satan's demons. Controversy is abroad in certain religious groups over this question, which threatens even to break fellowship between Christians and churches. How tragic. Satan likes nothing better than to get a good, hot controversy going over his work. He surely must stand by and laugh while the controversy does his work for him.

There are degrees of problems which all believers can have with Satan and his world of darkness. The levels of intensity with which we wrestle are very obvious. This is perhaps the best way of considering how much a believer can suffer from his enemy's activity. With this in mind, let's approach the believer's warfare by considering various levels of warfare.

DEMONIC OPPRESSION

All believers, as has been stated earlier, are under attack from Satan's forces. We are a target for him to oppose, hinder, hurt, and destroy if at all possible. From outside of our person, these powers can draw very near to inject their temptations into our minds, to tamper with our emotions, to soften and condition our wills, and to assault our bodies. Job took quite a beating from Satan's forces, and it was all from outside.

All Christians must face this Satanic, demonic oppression in varying degrees. The oppression can be so intense and so great, one may almost despair of standing. It takes all-out application of our spiritual resources to stand even against this oppressive assault (Eph 6:13). Spiritual victory over Satan requires full employment of our victory in Christ, regardless of the level or intensity of conflict we face.

DEMONIC OBSESSION

Care must be exercised here to define terms. *Demonic obsession* traditionally has meant the subject's uncontrollable preoccupation with demonic forces or phenomena. This demonic activity frequently pervades the subject's attention and pursuits in a dictating manner.

It is something less than total commitment or ownership, but is a step in that direction. A Christian who has of his own will developed overt curiosity about the occult, or in other ways has habitually given ground to Satan, may find himself demonically obsessed as traditionally defined. However, attention should be called to a more intense level of attack upon a believer which is common among believers today. It is obsessive in nature, but varies from the traditional concept of demonic obsession in that it need not be caused by sin or ground-giving on the part of the believer.

For committed believers, there does seem to be a level of conflict with Satan's forces that goes beyond ordinary oppressive warfare with Satan's forces. Keep in mind that the word *obsession* at this point is being used to describe a more intense level of demonic attack which may be experienced by all believers. A New Testament example of this more intense level of a believer's warfare is to be found in the life of the apostle Paul as related in 2 Corinthians 12:7-10:

> To keep me from becoming conceited because of these surpassingly great revelations, there was given to me a thorn in my flesh, a messenger of Satan, to torment me. Three times I pleaded with the Lord to take it away from me. But he said to me, 'My grace is sufficient for you, for my power is made perfect in weakness.' Therefore, I will boast all the more gladly about my weaknesses, so that Christ's power may rest on me. That is why, for Christ's sake, I delight in weaknesses, in insults, in hardships, in persecutions, in difficulties. For when I am weak, then I am strong.

This passage provides some keen insight into our warfare with Satan and some of God's sovereign purpose in allowing the attack to come.

The apostle had been greatly blessed of God. He had enjoyed a trip into glory so transcendent and superlative that he couldn't talk about it. One of God's most difficult tasks with any of us is to get us ready to be blessed of Him. Pride puffs us up so quickly that we soon become useless to God's work, and discipline must come. The intense or obsessive nature of this messenger of Satan in no way indicates that the apostle had unconfessed sin in his life or was in some other way involved in evildoing. It is true that greater intensity of Satan's activity against us can be the result of such unconfessed sin, but in Paul's case there was a sovereign purpose of God in allowing Satan's troubling, obsessive work.

Our Lord took care of any temptation to pride in Paul's case by removing just enough of His holy hedge to allow a messenger of Satan, some kind of "thorn in the flesh" to intensely harass and trouble Paul. The affliction or obsessive problem was so disagreeable and troublesome to Paul that he intensely sought the Lord on three occasions to remove this messenger of Satan from his life. The answer from the Lord came in the form of a quieting promise from the Lord that His grace would be sufficient and that God's strength is made perfect as we see our own weakness. This tremendous passage affords great comfort to anyone undergoing a severe time of battle with Satan. We must see that God has a sovereign purpose in a believer's life, even during Satan's intense battle. He is working out His will in our lives, even when on the surface it looks like Satan is winning.

The obvious evidence in this account is that this steady, throbbing battle with Satan was above the ordinary warfare that Paul knew so well. This was a steady, constant, nagging problem in a particular area and was a higher level of intense conflict with Satan.

DEMONIC POSSESSION

The third level is the question of demonic possession. Can a believer have a demon or demons actually enter into his person (body, soul, or spirit) and control him? This will require some careful looking at the biblical perspective of so-called demon possession. We must see first of all that the word *possession*, though in our English tradition, is not an expression of the original language. The way the

Greek language handles this problem is to call such people demoniacs or that they "had a demon."

It is obvious that these people Jesus and others delivered had demons in them. They spoke through the afflicted person's mouth and were commanded to come out. Such a possessed person is controlled by this evil spirit power and usually exercises his activity in the person at his will. The person is not himself. Some other being exercises ownership over him.

UNBELIEVERS POSSESSED.

Much is being written about this subject today. Many books by evangelical writers are providing ample illustrations and examples of the reality of people being taken over by demons. Such books must be read with care and prayer. Some which go into the lurid details of seances and Satan worship sessions should be avoided. Curiosity about evil is never good. The apostle Paul stated that some things are too evil to even mention and are better left unsaid and unread (Eph 5:12). We must be careful that idle curiosity to look into these subjects does not in itself give Satan an advantage against us.

Willing possession. This kind of problem is a growing and very deadly, dangerous situation. More and more people in our day are becoming actively interested in the occult world. They desire to be taken over by spirit powers that they might conduct seances, pronounce curses, become a witch, or secure some other supernatural condition. Many of these who engage in this kind of human tragedy are fully aware that they are being controlled and possessed by demonic, satanic powers. They desire a supernatural experience from Satan, thinking that it will bring them power, position, or some other thing they deem good in their scale of values. Some even desire those so-called good spirits who will enable them to do white magic or beneficial supernatural deeds for mankind. It all comes from the same deceiver, however, whether it is white or black magic, and it results in bondage to Satan.

Unwilling possession. It is obvious from life as well as from Scripture that many people become unwillingly possessed. Some are little children, as is evidenced in Mark 9:21 when the demon entered into the child whom the father brought to Jesus for help. Many others suffer terribly from these cruel, wicked powers of Satan. They long to be free, and their families long to help them get free.

How does this unwilling control come about? None of us can know all of the answers to such a searching question, but here are some possibilities. One way is when a person gives ground to Satan by willful, even though ignorant, dabbling into various areas of sin. Any occult investigation seems particularly dangerous. Perhaps this is why in the Old Testament, the Lord prescribed death to any of His people who became involved in sorcery or witchcraft. Please note these words to stay clear of any involvement into anything having to do with the occult. Ouija boards, party seances, levitation, tarot cards, fortune tellers, tea leaf readers, and the like, are not just fakes to be dabbled in for amusement. They belong to Satan's realm and should be avoided. I've been involved long enough in counseling troubled folk who are battling Satan to know that even the most nonchalant dabbling in the occult can spell disastrous results. Drug usage, drunkenness, sexual licentiousness, and lying are other sins of human depravity which may open one's life to unusual Satanic takeover.

What some have called transference is another way unwilling demonic possession of unbelievers may come. Demonic powers want to stay in families and ancestral blood lines. An ancestor who gives place to Satan is not only hurting himself, but he is opening the door of grave harm to his children, grandchildren, and on down the line. This ground of transference would seem to account for little children having to endure this invasion of the powers of darkness.

Believers and possession. It is my conviction that no believer can be possessed by an evil spirit in the same sense that an unbeliever can. In fact, I reject this term altogether when talking about a believer's problem with the powers of darkness. A believer may be afflicted or even controlled in certain areas of his being, but he can never be owned or totally controlled as an unbeliever can.

The moment a person becomes a believer, the Holy Spirit brings birth to his spirit. "Flesh gives birth to flesh, but the Spirit gives birth to spirit" (John 3:6, NIV). The spirit of the Christian is reborn, regenerated, possessed, and sealed by the Holy Spirit in a way not enjoyed by the rest of man's being as yet. The spirit of man thus reborn, becomes the Holy Spirit's unique center of control and operation within man.* I do not believe that any wicked spirit can ever invade a believer's spirit. The Holy Spirit's work of new birth and His sealing presence within the spirit of man seem to preclude any presence of wicked spirit control of that part of man's being. I realize that those who hold a dichotomist view of man's being will not find this explanation acceptable, but it has helped my own understanding of this deepest level of a believer's battle with Satan.

A believer's soul, containing his mind, his will, and his emotions, is in process of being transformed by his growth in grace and the maturing work of the fullness of the Holy Spirit in his life (Ro 12:1-2). The regeneration and rebirth of the spirit of man is an instantaneous miracle that takes place the moment he believes. As I understand it, the spirit is as reborn at the moment of a person's conversion as it will ever be. His full soul and body transformation into the likeness of Christ, however, is a lifelong process and will only really be complete when he receives his resurrected, glorified body. Transformation requires the involvement and active participation of his mind, his will, his emotions, and his body. The combination of faith in God's provisions and processes, and submission to the Holy Spirit is necessary to this ongoing process of transformation.

*For a helpful study of the unique relationship of the believer's spirit to his soul and body, see Watchman Nee, *The Spiritual Man*, 3 vols. (New York: Christian Fellowship, 1968).

It is in this area of our own responsibility to growth in Christ that the activity of Satan concentrates against us. If I believe a lie of Satan and act upon that lie in some behavior, I give him ground against me. If I will to give in to some fleshly sin problem and fail to claim my victory over the flesh, I give ground to Satan. This enemy is ever attempting to gain some claim against us which in essence means that with our mind or will or emotion, or all three, we have rejected God's truth and have followed Satan's lie. The deceiving may be so subtle as to be an unconscious thing. This is like opening the door of your life and letting the thief who is going to rob and hurt you have a place in your life (Eph 4:27). Satan's worker will try to get more helpers to move in, and they will begin to try to dictate to you in certain given areas how you will feel, think or act. They will even try to increase their areas of hold through more deceivings and more lessening of your own will to the substitution of theirs. These are real spirit beings who have minds, wills, and emotions of their own. They desire to cause you to feel with their emotions, think their thoughts, and will to do what is their will. They will be so clever as to make it almost impossible to separate your own mind, will and emotions from theirs.

In helping people get free of deep demonic affliction, I have seen people radically changed when the dictating powers are dispatched to the place the Lord Jesus Christ sends them. The thoughts that torment their minds cease, the feelings that surged through their emotions are gone, and the will that controlled their will is broken. The believer thus delivered enjoys a new freedom to submit himself to the control and work of the Holy Spirit's fullness.

The best way to describe this problem is to recognize it as the most intensive form of demonic affliction a Christian can suffer. The only way this intensive problem can be resolved is to bring the weapons of our warfare directly against these intruders and force them to leave one's presence. Sometimes aggressive use of prayer, the application of the doctrines of the Word of God, praise to the Lord, and other active employment of all we have in Christ is sufficient to break the hold and dictates of any such demonic affliction. At other times, straightforward challenge and taking authority over such intruding powers may be necessary. The methods of spiritual warfare against the kingdom of darkness will be discussed in later chapters. It is the purpose of our study here to see that the demonic forces of Satan can afflict Christians so deeply as to harm their bodies, dictate to them certain attitudes of mind, certain feelings of emotions, and certain expressions of will that are all Satan's doings. To call this possession, in my judgment, is unwise and fails to recognize the difference between a believer's afflictions from Satan and an unbeliever being possessed, signifying total control and ownership.

We must realize, however, that this enemy called Satan can gain a great advantage over us as believers. This advantage can only be broken by the employing of the weapons of our warfare aggressively against an enemy who we are willing to admit is controlling us in any given area.

An account out of my own ministry illustrates the practical application of these truths. This incident took place several years ago as God was leading me into more understanding of satanic warfare. My phone rang at about 2:00 A.M.

"Hello. You don't know me and I don't know you, but I know what you and your church stand for. Unless you can help me, I'm determined to end it all tonight. I have no idea why I'm calling you. I've been drinking, trying to get up courage to kill myself."

Sensing a serious problem and a state of mind capable of suicide, I asked him if he wouldn't like to at least talk about what was hurting him so deeply that he wanted to end his life.

"That won't do any good," he said. "No one can help with my kind of problem. I've been to Dr. _____ (naming a well-known psychiatrist in our area) and Dr. _____, (naming another psychiatrist). I'm a born-again Christian. I've tried to overcome my problem. Oh! How I've tried, but it's no use. I've counseled with several different pastors and Christian counselors, but no one can help anyone with my problem."

"Would you like to share your problem with me?" I inquired.

"No, that won't help. I just want to know, if I take my life, will I still go to heaven? I'm not going to fight it anymore. I can't live with the guilt; and I hate it, I hate it. I'm a professional man, and if my associates knew, I'd be discharged in disgrace. I've prayed and I've prayed, but that hasn't helped."

I responded by quoting some Scripture and with some words assuring him of God's understanding, willingness to forgive and to help us when we're sincerely reaching out. Then with prayerful and careful tone I asked, "Have you ever considered that this bondage might be demonic?"

There was silence for a few moments on the other end of the line. He later told me that when I asked that question it was as if a surge of rage ebbed and flowed in him, but deep inside his being the first spark of hope he'd had in many a year was born.

"But I'm a Christian," he protested. "It couldn't be demons, could it?"

I explained that I was not sure that it was, but from my limited experience, I felt it could be. I prayed with him, binding up all of Satan's powers that were seeking to destroy him, and though he refused to give me his name, I suggested he call me the next day. He did so, and we shared some counseling times together. The problem bore many symptoms of demon activity. At that time, I was not yet willing to tackle the challenge on my own and sent him to a friend of mine who had experienced victory over such demonic control. Four wicked powers revealed their presence. One of them had a name which was the same as the man's problem. Another wicked power's name was suicide. These powers were commanded to leave and go to the pit, which they did. A marvelous deliverance from his problem resulted, and a whole new life opened to him, which he is now enjoying with his wife and family.

There is victory over all enemies we face to be found in our Lord Jesus Christ. Let us claim it and use it.

7

THERE'S STILL A PLACE FOR OBJECTIVE DOCTRINE

"All scripture is given by inspiration of God, and is profitable for doctrine, for reproof, for correction, for instruction in righteousness: that the man of God may be perfect, thoroughly furnished unto all good works" (2 Ti 3:16-17, KJV).

RECENTLY I received a call from a man who attends a sister church in our city. He'd gone to his pastor, a close personal friend of mine, about his problems, and his pastor suggested that he talk with me. His story was typical of ever-increasing numbers of new believers. Prior to his conversion, he had lived a life of sinful tragedy and empty failure. Drug experimentation, sexual licentiousness, and involvement with varied occult practices had all been a part of his worldly life. Finding Christ as Lord and Saviour had brought great joy, release, and meaning into his life and home. How wonderful it is to see the saving grace of our Lord changing the lives of so many who have been so deeply trapped in the vise of sin.

After his conversion he began to experience spiritual problems that seemed beyond his capacity to cope. Compulsive and explosive emotional outbursts of rage against loved ones and blasphemous thoughts against God and others were the most pronounced problems. Try as he would, he seemed completely incapable of handling these problems. He could see himself and his dear ones being destroyed and his witness for Christ devoid of the testimony of victory. Through his pastor's preaching he had come to see that his problems might well be demonic and satanic affliction. In desperation he was asking, "What do I do now?"

This man's question is being asked by countless numbers of believers today. This is a very vital and practical question that must have answers. For a believer to become aware that he is defeated by Satan's warfare is self-defeating and fear-producing if he doesn't know what to do about it. It will be the purpose of this and the following chapters to suggest practical steps to take in warfare against Satan. Faithful usage of the victory purchased and achieved for us by the Lord Jesus Christ always defeats Satan's warfare against us.

Basic to all victory of the believer over Satan is the absolute truth of Bible doctrine. In the account of His wilderness temptation, our Lord provided us the key to defeating Satan when he or his demons confront us. Each time Satan tempted him or misapplied a statement of the Word, our Lord replied, "It is written," and then correctly quoted and applied the truth of God (See Mt 4:1-11).

How greatly important it is to see that Satan backs off from nothing but the absolute truth and fact of God's Word. As has been previously stated, Satan finds our emotions, wishes, and sincere desires no problem for him to defeat. With all of my heart, I can want to love and serve the Lord and not be defeated by Satan, but I'll fail in my sincerity if I do not use the truth of God against Satan and to my own strengthening. Seeing this truth is perhaps the single greatest key in warfare against Satan.

It is not enough to know sound doctrine. I must use it and apply it in my daily walk. Every truth of God's Word is given to us not just to know but to use for God's glory and our victory. That is what 2 Timothy 3:16-17 really means.

How, then, do I use the sound truths of God's Word? Our faith is a living, vital experiential faith that is to be lived out in daily affairs. It does me little good experientially to know that I'm justified by faith unless I use that truth to glorify God and to walk in victory.

One of the best ways to employ sound Bible doctrine is in what I like to call doctrinal praying. Insight into this truth has continued to grow in my own life until large blocks of time in my prayer time are devoted to claiming and applying the mighty doctrines of the Word of God. Since God opened my eyes to the importance of this aggressive use of doctrine in my prayer life and daily walk, my own victory in Christ has been greatly benefited and enhanced.

Doctrinal praying is the practice of praying or applying the objective, absolute truths of the Word of God as the hope and basis of resolving our prayer burden. God loves for us to pray His Word back to Him, claiming His attributes, promises, and redemptive work as the ground of our faith that He will answer. It is obvious, for example, that many of the prayers of the psalmist flow out of the subjective feelings, failures, and emotional needs of the one praying. The hope and solution of the prayer burden, however, is always based upon the objective absolutes of God's attributes and character as revealed in His Word (see Ps 51; 86; 102). The hope of resolving subjective problems and needs will always rest with the applying of God's objective truth to meet those problems and needs.

Anyone who works with those who are troubled with deep demonic affliction knows the vital importance of wise use of God's truth against demonic powers. Recently I was endeavoring to help a young man get free of demonic powers that had a very destroying hold upon his life. Through his faculties I was in direct confrontation with a snarling, cruel, crude, vulgar demon that had taken the same name as this young man's last name. This wicked power was very talkative. He constantly threatened and insulted me, the young man, and another person who was working with me in the confrontation. After taking back ground he was claiming against the young man, I kept commanding him to leave and go where the Lord Jesus Christ would send him. He was very obstinate in refusing to go. I kept quoting the truth of God against him, but even though he was weakening, he still refused to go. We were all near the point of exhaustion when finally I quoted the promise of our Lord, "Where two or three are gathered together in my name, there am I in the midst of them" (Mt 18:20, KJV).

After quoting this verse, I said, "This is the very truth of God. The Lord Jesus Christ is here. Dear Saviour, this wicked spirit is insulting You, and he's insulting us, Your servants. He refuses to leave at our command. I ask You now in Your presence here to put Your holy hand against him and to send him where You want him to go." Almost immediately, a great cry came out of the young man's mouth, and he was immediately delivered from that destroying power. The point I want you to see is that all of our hard work sincerity and effort was not sufficient. Only the absolute truth of God applied against the enemy prevailed.

More will be said in chapter nine about boldly confronting the intrusion of darkness into believers' lives. I share this experience to illustrate the vast importance of using doctrinal truth against Satan.

Doctrinal praying should occupy much of our daily prayer time. It must be used in praise, petition, and intercession. Herein lies one of God's greatest provisions for our prayer life. Examine the Lord's Prayer and other prayers recorded in the Word of God to see how much of doctrinal truth is contained in the prayers. It is a tragedy to discover how often the typical prayer rests on worn-out cliches and emotional desires and wishes. How little the average Christian seems to know about resting his petitions, praise, and intercessions upon the great revealed truths of God.

Since it is purposed in this book to give practical help, let me share with you what I consider to be a doctrinal prayer. Each believer will need to develop his own approach within his own personality and gifts, but I trust the practical use of doctrine will come through in this written prayer.

Dear Lord and heavenly Father. Humbly I approach the God and Father of our Lord Jesus Christ, the God of Abraham, Isaac, and Jacob, the God of promise, hope, love, and grace. I come before You in the merit, the holiness, and the righteousness of the Lord Jesus Christ. I appropriate by faith the blessed ministry of the Holy Spirit to intercede for me and in me during this time of prayer. I desire to pray only in the Spirit.

I praise You that I am united with the Lord Jesus Christ in all of His life and work. By faith I desire to enter into the victory of the incarnation of my Lord today. I appropriate by faith the victory He achieved for me in living His sinlessly perfect life as a human being. I claim all of His perfection and holy living. I invite Him to live His victory in me today. Thank You, Lord Jesus Christ, that You experienced all temptations I experience and yet never sinned. Thank You for defeating in Your incarnation all temptations and attacks that Satan and his kingdom were able to address against You. I claim Your victory over Satan as my victory today.

I enter by faith into the mighty work of the crucifixion of my Lord. Thank You that through the blood of Jesus Christ there is not only cleansing from the penalty and guilt of sin but moment-by-moment cleansing, permitting me to fellowship with You. Thank You that the work of the cross brings Satan's work to nothing. Deliberately and by faith, I bring all of the work of my Lord on Calvary directly against Satan's workings in my life. I will accept in my life only what comes by way of the cross of Christ. I chose to die to the old man. I count him to be dead with Christ on the cross. Grant to me the discernment and wisdom to see when the old man attempts to resurrect his activity in my life.

I enter by faith into the full power and authority of my Lord's resurrection. I desire to walk in the newness of life which is mine through my Lord's resurrection. Lead me ever more into a deep understanding of the power of the resurrection. I bring the mighty truth of my Lord's victory over the grave against all of Satan's workings against Your will and plan for my life. The enemy is defeated in my life because I am united with the Lord Jesus Christ in the victory of His resurrection.

By faith I appropriate and enter today into my union with the Lord Jesus Christ in His ascension. I rejoice that my Lord displayed openly His victory over all principalities and powers as He ascended into glory through the very realm of the prince of the power of the air. I rejoice that He is seated in victory far above all principalities and powers and that I am seated there with Him. Because of my union with my Saviour, I affirm my full authority and position of victory over Satan and all of his kingdom of darkness.

By faith I enter into the benefit and blessedness of my union with Christ in His glorification. It is my joy to choose to obey Him who is my Shepherd. I ask for You to lead me in Your path today. As my great High Priest, I appropriate your high priestly work into my life today. Thank You, Lord Jesus Christ, for interceding for me and being my advocate with the heavenly Father. Thank You for watching over me and leading me, that Satan may gain no advantage over me. Grant me wisdom to discern all of the devil's deceivings and temptations.

By faith I invite the Person of the Holy Spirit to bring the fullness of all of His person and my Lord's work into all areas of my being. I ask the Holy Spirit to fill my mind, my will, and my emotions with His control. I choose for Him to bring all parts of my being into wholeness and submission to the Lordship of Christ. I give my body in all of its parts and appetites to the Holy Spirit's control and transformation. *I desire that He enable my spirit to be in fellowship with the Father, the Son, and the Holy Spirit throughout this day. I offer up this prayer to the heavenly Father in the name of the Lord Jesus Christ with thanksgiving. Amen.*

I end this example of prayer at this point, trusting that what is meant by doctrinal praying begins to open up to you. Further application of doctrine in prayer will be developed in the next chapter. I trust that you will see the great opportunity for worship and praise to God that such prayer affords, as well as gaining insight into its importance for victory over Satan.

In my early ministry, a man I knew died after living the life of a pauper. He scrounged in garbage cans for food, discarded clothing, or anything else of value. He lived in a garage part of the time, and tried to impose on his brother the rest of the time. One day he suffered a sudden heart attack, and after a brief time in the hospital, he died. After his death, it was discovered that this man had well over one hundred thousand dollars concealed in various places. He had much wealth which he was free to use because it was his, but he failed to use it.

Believers also have a vast resource of wealth and riches in the grace and gifts bestowed upon them in the Lord Jesus Christ. These precious truths are ours. They are immutably and eternally made ours in Christ. Power, position, authority, total victory over Satan's world belongs to us. It remains only for us to lay hold of our promises and position and bring it consistently and strongly to focus against the devil's work, and to claim God's full will and purpose for His saving us.

The believer's victory over Satan is absolute when he uses the great truths of God to defeat him. God's Word cannot fail.

Let us sum up our ways to victory over Satan. The Word sets forth at least four active ways in which we are responsible to defeat Satan's work against us. Let's bring them together here that we may see how vitally they are related to sound doctrine. First we must resist him (Ja 4:7; 1 Pe 5:8-9). Resisting Satan means that we actively submit to God and come against Satan and all of his work against us, stedfast in the faith. This simply means a steady, consistent bringing of the great truths of the faith against Satan. It is not improper but very biblical to address yourself against Satan, resisting him with the doctrinal truth of our faith. Address him like this when warring against him:

> Satan, I resist you and all of your workers in the Person and power of the Lord Jesus Christ. I submit to the Lordship and control of the Lord Jesus, and I bring the power of my Lord's incarnation, His crucifixion, His resurrection, His ascension, His glorification and His second coming directly to focus against you and all of your work against me. I claim my union with the Lord Jesus Christ, and I resist you; I resist you, and I force you to flee from before the truth of God.

The second important way to victory over Satan is to be filled with the Holy Spirit. The ground of the believer's victory includes this active work of the blessed Comforter in our lives. In Luke 4:1 as our Lord was led forth to meet Satan in that most powerful wilderness encounter, we learn that He was filled with the Holy Spirit. In His humanity our Lord shows us the way to our victory over Satan. The Holy Spirit's fullness is vital to deliverance and continuing victory.

A special plan of our victory over Satan is found in Revelation 12:11. "And they overcame him by the blood of the Lamb, and by the word of their testimony" (KJV).

Hebrews 2:14b-15, states, "That through death he [Christ] might destroy [bring to naught] him that had the power of death, that is, the devil; and deliver them who through fear of death were all their lifetime subject to bondage" (KJV).

The death of Christ and particularly the shed blood of Calvary spelled an awful defeat for Satan. By the Word of our testimony as we bring the blood of Christ directly against Satan, we overcome him. Words spoken aggressively concerning our faith in Christ's death and His shed blood are a mighty weapon to use in our warfare.

The fourth way to victory is to put on the armor of the Christian. This has been discussed in the previous chapter, but to stress its daily importance again seems wise in this bringing together of our weapons against Satan. In these chapters we have sought to see the ways in which the world, the flesh, and the devil attack us. We have also sought to look at the biblical answers which spell the defeat of each enemy. It is obvious that there is some overlapping and working together of these enemies. Satan's activity stirs up the activity and intensity of the flesh and the world system. The potential for wickedness and the actual wickedness of man's depraved nature is always there, but Satan knows how to stir its activity to his purpose.

The question now remains as to how I am to determine if my problems with temptations are of the world, the flesh, or the devil. How will I know if my problem has gone beyond a fleshly one and has become a demonic problem? How will I know if my problem is more than a worldly temptation and has a satanic power dictating to me?

The answer to this seems again to rest in this matter of sound doctrine. If I earnestly seek the defeat of one of the fleshly sins through the biblical methods previously discussed but without results, if I find a worldly temptation defeating me even though I am aggressively using my provided victory over the world, I must now consider the fact that my problem well may be some demonic hold of Satan's powers which must be broken.

Spiritual warfare includes a continual, active aggressive warfare against all three enemies. I must seek to understand which enemy I am facing that I might apply God's remedy against that enemy. It is not good to blame our own fleshly depravity on the world or even Satan. Truth demands objective facing of the facts, followed by subjective application of God's truth to the need. All victory rests in the truth of God. I must not trust in emotional fanfare. I must not trust in sensational gimmicks. My victory rests only in the "thus saith the Lord." Sound doctrine is absolutely essential to victorious spiritual warfare over Satan.

Heavenly Father, I rejoice in the immutable, absolute truth of Your Word. In Your grace, keep me from knowing only the letter of truth and sound doctrine. Let it enter my spirit, let it control my mind, let it stabilize and energize my emotions. I will to apply Your truth aggressively and to depend upon its power to defeat all of my enemies. Through the intercessory work of the Holy Spirit and in the name of my Lord Jesus Christ, I thank You for hearing this petition. Amen.

8

AGGRESSIVE PRAYER WINS AGAIN

"For though we walk in the flesh, we do not war according to the flesh, for the weapons of our warfare are not of the flesh, but divinely powerful for the destruction of fortresses. We are destroying speculations and every lofty thing raised up against the knowledge of God, and we are taking every thought captive to the obedience of Christ" **(2 Co 10:3-5, NASB).**

THE PARAPHRASED *Living Bible* brings to these words the fresh graphic interpretation of today's language. "It is true that I am an ordinary, weak human being, but I don't use human plans and methods to win my battles. I use God's mighty weapons, not those made by man, to knock down the devil's strongholds. These weapons can break down every proud argument against God and every wall that can be built to keep men from finding him. With these weapons I can capture rebels and bring them back to God, and change them into men whose hearts' desire is obedience to Christ."

A believer who brings to grasp the tremendous power of his spiritual weaponry through understanding passages like this will find a new joy in prayer. Prayer is the chief means by which our faith expresses itself. Prayer is the chief means by which we employ and appropriate the victory which is ours over all principalities and powers. The mighty resources in prayer remain yet to be tapped in most believers' lives.

God gave a new insight on prayer and a precious work of His Spirit in my own heart during the time the Chicago Seven Conspiracy trial was taking place in Chicago. The events of that long, semi-notorious trial provided headline news stories in Chicago and for the most part, over the nation. I was listening to the news one day as I drove up to one of our Chicago area hospitals to make a call on one of our members. The newscaster stated that one of the most well-known of the Chicago Seven defendants had been taken to the hospital with viral pneumonia. It so happened that the hospital was the very one I was visiting. I got out of the car, wondering where he could be in the vast complex of buildings that make up that particular hospital.

I made my call, sharing a time in the Word and prayer before leaving. As I was about to go, the patient I was visiting said to me, "By the way, we have a celebrity across the hall. John Smith [not his real name] is here with pneumonia." I expressed my surprise, and after a few moments of conversation, I left without further thought. As I waited for the elevator, suddenly the Spirit of God moved on my heart. There came a great awareness that the Lord wanted me to speak to this celebrated defendant about God's love for him. I quickly discarded the idea as just an overworking of my imagination and the powers of suggestion. However, as the elevator descended, once again this very strong impression returned that I was to go and relate to this man that God loved him and desired to give him a new life in Christ. Once again, I quickly rejected the impression, thinking perhaps it was my own idea.

I started to walk across the lobby of the hospital toward my car when for a third time the Holy Spirit moved upon me. This time the message was unmistakably clear. The Lord willed that I should relate to this man God's love for him. A refusal to obey would be a serious affront to the Holy Spirit. Fear and trembling visited my soul. It is not common to my nature to visit such well-known personages of some notoriety to tell them God loves them. Not giving myself any time for reconsideration, I immediately responded and said, "All right, Lord, I'll go; but You'll have to open the door for my going and give me the words to say." I walked back through the lobby and up to the floor I'd just left. I went to the hospital station serving that wing and wondered what I'd say to the head nurse. When she asked me what I wanted, I related to her the story as you've just read it. She looked at me in dumb amazement. She didn't know what to say. She was about to tell me my request was impossible when a resident physician who was listening said, "Just a minute, nurse. I'll go ask him if he'll see this pastor."

In a few moments he returned and said, "He'll see you in ten minutes when his attorney leaves." I was very pleased for the time delay. I quickly went to the room of my Christian brother and asked him to pray. I hurriedly called my wife, asking her to pray and to call others to pray.

The ten minutes went quickly, and I was in the room talking to this man. After introducing myself, I wondered, *What do I say now?* Then, the Lord stepped in. In a most wonderful way, our Lord moved upon me, and for nearly thirty minutes I was able to share of God's love, mercy, and transforming power through Jesus Christ our Lord. The hardness of his heart and the spiritual blindness upon him was as great as I have ever seen, but he thanked me for coming and as I left, he remarked, "Say some prayers for me in this trial."

This experience moved me greatly as I was driving home. The loving outreach of God to hardened, rebellious men moved me to tears. Since that experience, God has moved often upon my heart to pray for this man. I believe in God's plan He is going to save this man. As I pen these words, his name is again in the headlines for seriously breaking the law. By faith, I see another headline one of these days telling of his dramatic conversion to Jesus Christ. I foresee a witness resulting, similar to that of the apostle Paul after his dramatic conversion.

I relate this story as a background to share with you an example of aggressive prayer in spiritual warfare. This example of warfare praying is meant to turn many believers to this kind of intercession for the many the Holy Spirit may place before you as His assignment. The name is fictitious, for obvious reasons.

Loving heavenly Father, in the name of our Lord Jesus Christ, I bring before You in prayer (John Smith). I ask for the Holy Spirit's guidance that I might pray in the Spirit as You have told me. I thank You, heavenly Father, that You have sovereign control over (John Smith). I thank You for the qualities of aggressiveness and leadership which I see that You have placed in this man. In the name of the Lord Jesus Christ and as a priest of God, I ask for mercy and forgiveness for the sins of (John Smith) by which he has grieved You. I plead the sufficiency of the blood of Christ to meet the full penalty his sins deserve. I claim back the ground of his life which he has given to Satan by believing the enemy's deception. In the name of the Lord Jesus Christ I resist all of Satan's activity to hold (John) in blindness and darkness. Exercising my authority which is given to me in my union with the Lord Jesus Christ, I pull down the strongholds which the kingdom of darkness has formed against (John). I smash and break and destroy all those plans formed against (John's) mind, his will, his emotions, and his body. I destroy in prayer the spiritual blindness and deafness that Satan keeps upon him. I invite the Holy Spirit of God to bring the fullness of His power to convict, to bring to repentance, and to lead (John) into faith in the Lord Jesus Christ as his Saviour. I cover him with the blood of the Lord Jesus Christ, and I break Satan's power to blind him to the truth of God.

Believing that Your Holy Spirit is leading me, I claim (John Smith) for You in the name of the Lord Jesus Christ, and I thank You for the answer to my prayer. In the name of the Lord Jesus Christ I joyfully lay this prayer before You in the worthiness of His completed work. Amen.

Aggressive warfare praying of this type represents one of the greatest needs of intercession in this day. There are multitudes about us who, though they may be notorious sinners, are some of the other sheep that our Lord says He must bring (see Jn 10:16). Willingness to pray with aggressive prayer of this type is mighty and powerful in setting them free. It is an exciting and joyful ministry to enter into this warfare of pulling down strongholds and watching the Holy Spirit work as the powers of darkness to blind are broken away.

This kind of aggressive warfare praying has almost limitless application in defeating Satan's power and to "capture rebels and bring them back to God, and change them into men whose heart's desire is obedience to Christ" (2 Co 10:5, TLB). Here are several practical applications of this truth.

Many dear Christian parents have broken hearts because of rebellious, sinbound children who seem to be in bondage to Satan. Much prayer often goes up expressing the brokenhearted disappointment, but there is too often a lack of application of the principles of warfare praying. I could share numerous illustrations of joyful results which have come from such praying.

Suppose you have a son who is rebellious and far from God. He's on drugs, living in immorality, and in every form of debased depravity. How would you claim 2 Corinthians 10:3-5 in this need? Let me suggest a practical illustration of prayer recommended to some Christian parents who saw such a son respond to Christ as a result of such praying.

I bow humbly before the heavenly Father to intercede for my son, John. I bring him before You in the name of the Lord Jesus Christ. I thank You that You have loved John with the love of Calvary. I thank You that You gave him to us to love and nurture in Christ. I ask You to forgive us for all of our failures to guide him in the way he ought to go. I am thankful that You are sovereign and can use even the depths of sin to which he is now enslaved to redound to your glory. I praise You for this great trial that humbles my heart before You.

Accepting my position of being "mighty through God to the pulling down of strong holds," I bring all of the work of the Lord Jesus Christ to focus directly against the powers of darkness that blind and bind John. I pray the victory of our Lord's incarnation, crucifixion, resurrection, ascension, and glorification directly against all of Satan's power in John's life. I bind up all powers of darkness set to destroying John, and I loose him from their blinding in the name of the Lord Jesus Christ. I invite the blessed Holy Spirit to move upon John's heart and to convict him of sin, of righteousness, and of judgment to come. In my priestly ministry, I confess John's sins unto You and plead Your compassionate mercy toward Him. I confess his yielding to all manner of fleshly sins which has given Satan such place in his life. I plead the blood of Christ over John's wickedness and wait upon the Holy Spirit to bring him to repentance, faith, and life in the Lord Jesus Christ. By faith I claim him for a life yielded to serve the true and living God in the name of the Lord Jesus Christ. Amen.

Satan will go to almost any lengths to divert the believer from warfare praying. A brilliant college senior came to see me one day about some very distressing problems she was facing. She related some of the terrifying dreams she endured, the compulsive acts, the vile thoughts, and other behavioral patterns which she hated. She told me of her background with certain occult involvements. The more she shared her story, the more I could see the bondage and concentration of Satan's attack.

This girl had been a believer for about one year. When first saved, the symptoms just described had greatly abated. As the days passed, she had gradually drifted into fleshly and worldly sins. Her problems now seemed even worse than they had been prior to her conversion. She was convinced that she was losing her mind. Carefully and gradually I led her into a study of the Word on the matter of Satan's person and work. It is not unusual for someone who is troubled by demonic attack to have a great fear of the subject. You must be very gentle and prayerful as you seek to communicate the victory the believer has in Christ over Satan's powers. If you bluster into the subject, the person you seek to help may draw back, and the enemy will use your good intentions to create fear. To some people, any thought that they might be having trouble with demonic forces is taken as an insult.

This college senior was able to grasp the truth of the Word on the subject of spiritual warfare with unusual facility. One of her projects of warfare against the forces of darkness troubling her was aggressive warfare prayer. I assigned her the responsibility of reading once a day the "warfare prayer" as it is found in chapter 11 of this book. My objective was to help her learn to claim the truths of God's Word and apply them against her enemies. She was a diligent and faithful counselee. Before classes each day she'd try to go through that warfare prayer. At first she could only go through half of it, and this would require thirty minutes' effort. Normally, a good reader could read the whole prayer aloud in eight minutes. The assault from the powers of darkness assigned against her was so intense she could scarcely read it. Dizziness, diverted attention, black spots before her eyes, and other physical and emotional attack was in constant evidence. This attack seemed to make her only more determined to be free, however, and the more she used her weapons of warfare, the weaker became the attack. Eventually she could go through the prayer as proficiently as anyone.

I relate this case to show how important aggressive warfare praying is to one's own spiritual life. It is important to be bold and direct in applying the weapons of our warfare to our own strengthening and to the enemy's defeat. The apostle Paul tells us to pray without ceasing. How important this is to meeting the intrusions of demonic assault and temptation.

A believer related to me how he had some horrifying thoughts of murder constantly intruding into his mind. Every time he'd see a knife when in the kitchen with his wife or children, a suggestion to grab the knife and stab his loved one would intrude his thoughts. Great guilt and fear ensued. "What kind of a person am I to have thoughts like these? How sinful and vile could a man be? Surely I must be losing my mind." How great can be the torment of one so tempted! As he learned about warfare praying, however, complete victory came very quickly. I share with you the kind of prayer I suggested he use, silently unto God, whenever such thoughts came.

Heavenly Father, I reject these thoughts of murder in the name of the Lord Jesus Christ. I recognize they are from the one You called a murderer from the beginning. I apply my union with the Lord Jesus Christ and His shed blood directly against the power of Satan causing these thoughts. I command him to leave my presence. I submit my mind, my will, and my emotions only to the Holy Spirit in the name of the Lord Jesus Christ. Amen.

A prayer of this type should be ready always to launch an aggressive attack against any messenger of Satan that dares to intrude into our lives.

One of the great assaults of the kingdom of darkness today is against marriage and the home. I believe that aggressive warfare prayer is essential to the building of harmonious, beautiful marriages according to the will of God. If Satan's kingdom can keep a husband and wife from loving each other according to God's will and way, he will not only ruin them, but will destroy their children's lives. The greatest thing any parent can give to his child is a home where Mother and Dad love each other with a beautiful, mature love from God. Husbands and wives ought to pray daily for God to bless their marriage. It is best if they pray together, but even one partner praying rightly is a powerful weapon against Satan's attack. If a couple comes to me for marriage counseling, their first assignment always is to begin to pray together. If they pray together, I know they are going to get help. If they do not, I know their marriage will continue to hit the skids, no matter how much counseling they get. The reason behind this thinking is that by the time a couple comes for counseling, it usually means that a prolonged battle has preceded. Much ground has been given to Satan, and recovery is possible only as our spiritual victory through the Lord Jesus is applied. Let me suggest a basic outline of prayer for a couple whose marriage is in trouble.

Loving heavenly Father, I thank You for Your perfect plan for our marriage. I know that a marriage functioning in Your will and blessing is fulfilling and beautiful. In the name of the Lord Jesus Christ, I bring our marriage before You that You might make it all You desire it to be. Please forgive me for my sins of failure in our marriage. [One may specify and enlarge confession.] In the name of the Lord Jesus Christ, I tear down all of Satan's strongholds designed to destroy our marriage. I break all relationships between us that have been established by Satan and his wicked spirits in the name of the Lord Jesus Christ. I will accept only the relationships established by You and the blessed Holy Spirit. I invite the Holy Spirit to enable me to relate to Mary in a manner that will meet her needs. I submit our conversation to You, that it may please You. I submit our physical relationship to You that it may enjoy your blessing. I submit our love to You that You may cause it to grow and mature. I desire to know and experience in marriage the fullness of Your perfect will. Open my eyes to see all areas where I am deceived. Open Mary's eyes to see any of Satan's deception upon her. Make our union to be the Christ-centered and blessed relationship You have designed in Your perfect will. I ask this in the name of the Lord Jesus Christ with thanksgiving. Amen.

There are times when it is important for us to stand in for another person in aggressive prayer. This is what intercessory prayer really is. We intercede in behalf of another. What can you do for someone who is under great bondage and has no awareness of his need or shows little desire or ability to get free? Employing warfare praying in his behalf can do much to break the enemy's hold upon his life.

This form of praying is particularly effective when exercised by a closely-tied relationship to the afflicted one. Examples are many in the Word where loved ones came to intercede with the Lord for the afflicted. The Lord ministered to the afflicted in direct response to the intercession (e.g., Mt 17:14-21).

Suppose you have a friend who shows symptoms of possible demonic bondage, yet he shows no desire to help himself or to have anyone else help him. You feel led of the Lord to help. What do you do? Bring him to Christ, just like they did in the days of our Lord's earthly ministry. You cannot bring him to the Lord Jesus Christ's physical presence, but you can bring him in persistent, intercessory warfare praying before the Lord. At the risk of being redundant, let me suggest another example of warfare praying for such a friend or loved one.

Heavenly Father, I bring before You and the Lord Jesus Christ one who is very dear to You and to me, Fred Smith. I have come to see that Satan is blinding and binding him in awful bondage. He is in such a condition that he cannot or will not come to You for help on his own. I stand in for him in intercessory prayer before Your throne. I draw upon the Person of the Holy Spirit that He may guide me to pray in wisdom, power, and understanding.

In the name of the Lord Jesus Christ, I loose Fred from the awful bondage the powers of darkness are putting upon him. I bind all powers of darkness set on destroying his life. I bind them aside in the name of the Lord Jesus Christ and forbid them to work. I bind up all powers of depression that are seeking to cut Fred off and imprison him in a tomb of despondency. I bring in prayer the focus of the Person and work of the Lord Jesus Christ directly upon Fred to his strengthening and help. I bring the mighty power of my Lord's incarnation, crucifixion, resurrection, ascension, and glorification directly against all forces of darkness seeking to destroy Fred. I ask the Holy Spirit to apply all of the mighty work of the Lord Jesus Christ directly against all forces of darkness seeking to destroy Fred.

I pray, heavenly Father, that You may open Fred's eyes of understanding. Remove all blindness and spiritual deafness from his heart. As a priest of God in Fred's life, I plead Your mercy over his sins of failure and rebellion. I claim all of his life united together in obedient love and service to the Lord Jesus Christ. May the Spirit of the living God focus His mighty work upon Fred to grant him repentance and to set him completely free from all that binds him.

In the name of the Lord Jesus Christ, I thank You for Your answer. Grant me the grace to be persistent and faithful in my intercessions for Fred, that You may be glorified through this deliverance, Amen.

Aggressive prayer is a mighty, mighty part of the believer's effectiveness in spiritual warfare. May our Lord grant a new vision of its importance and effectiveness in fighting the good fight. A fascinating study can be made of the great prayers of the Bible in seeing how aggressively intercession was made in behalf of others. It is obvious that some of these prayers were lifted to God's throne in behalf of others who were unable or unwilling to pray. Nehemiah aggressively confessed the sins of the children of Israel (Neh 1:6-7). Daniel entered into a stand in travail for his nation in Daniel 9, as he confessed the sins of those he loved before God. Abraham pled for Lot in Sodom, who was vexing his righteous soul with the sins of the city. The apostle Paul reveals his prayers for those he loved in his epistles. Moses pled for God's mercy in behalf of the unworthy and rebellious people he led, and God heard and spared. What a privilege to enter into warfare prayer in behalf of others who may display no desire to pray for themselves, but who reap the benefit and respond as we pray.

9

BOLD CONFRONTATION MAY BE NEEDED

"And he asked him, What is thy name? And he answered, saying, my name is Legion: for we are many" (Mk 5:9, KJV).

THIS VERSE reveals that our Lord confronted wicked spirits boldly and demanded that they reveal their wicked presence and work in the lives of people. They, in turn, responded to His commands, and in so doing acknowledged His full authority over them.

Believers, united with the Lord Jesus Christ in all of His person and work, have the same authority to claim and use that which our Lord used against wicked spirits. J. A. MacMillan's book, *The Authority of the Believer,* expounds the principles of the believer's authority set forth in the epistle to the Ephesians. This is one of the finest expositions upon the subject and basis of the believer's authority that I have ever read. In this study, MacMillan states:

> It has been pointed out more than once in this study that the authority of which we are speaking is the portion of every believer. It is not a special gift imparted in answer to prayer, but the inherent right of the child of God because of

his elevation with Christ to the right hand of the Father. He has become, through the rich mercy of God, an occupant of the Throne of the Lord, with all that it implies in privilege and responsibility. This elevation took place potentially at the resurrection of the Lord and because of the believer's inclusion in Him. The elevation is wholly of the wisdom and grace of the Father. We do not 'climb the heavenly steeps' by any act of faith or devotion on our part. It is ours simply to recognize the fact of this position, and to take our place in humble acceptance, giving all the glory and honor to God.*

The believer's authority is truly a settled fact. God our heavenly Father has planned it so; our Lord Jesus Christ declared it so; and the work of the Holy Spirit makes it so. It remains for believers to act upon this powerful truth.

For too many years, believers in the Western world have shown tragic temerity in any bold use of their authority in Christ. Even the most devoted pastors and Christian leaders have joined the ranks of those reticent to face any demonic power in a head-on confrontation. The results are appalling. Any people who are troubled with demons are ignored or even pushed away from any help they are entitled to receive from our Lord Jesus Christ.

As I approach this delicate subject, I am fully aware of the fear, uncertainty, and reluctance of most evangelical believers to get involved in any direct confrontation with demons. The excesses and extremism of so-called faith healers in this area is well known. Most of us do not want to be identified with such extremism. Some of us may fear that the evangelical hatchet will fall if we dare to venture into an area considered unsafe in the evangelical spectrum of practice. But perhaps the most universal reason why biblically-sound believers avoid confrontation with demonic powers is fear of the unknown. We just wouldn't know what to do or how to proceed in such a facedown with darkness. It will be the purpose of this chapter to try

*J. A. MacMillan, *The Authority of the Believer* (Harrisburg: Christian Pubns., n.d.), pp. 13-14.

to remove some of that fear. I trust that God also may call believers to see the importance of using their authority in Christ.

I want to identify very personally with those who may be facing severe satanic and demonic assault by relating the results of a confrontation with darkness which took place in my own family. As I relate this experience, I prayerfully trust that it will eliminate some of the fear and ignite expectant faith in many hearts.

As I have mentioned often in this book, we all face close wrestlings with the powers of darkness (Eph 6:10-18). Sometimes they come very close, and they are never more potent than when they touch our children. I find that many Christian parents absolutely refuse to admit that their children could be troubled by the forces of darkness. They would interpret such an admission as a reversion back into the dark fears of paganism. They don't know exactly how or why, but they are sure that their children must be absolutely safe from any intrusion of demons against them. I know whereof I speak, because I too was a part of that large segment of the evangelical world. It would have been easier to admit that my child had cancer or even was mentally ill than to admit that she was troubled with demonic affliction. I praise God that this isn't so anymore. Our family now looks back upon the whole experience I am about to relate as one of the greatest happenings in our home. Our growth in grace and appreciation of the victory which is ours in our Lord is experientially rooted to a depth we had never known before.

For several years, our youngest daughter had been troubled periodically with ill-defined fears. Physical nausea and colitis symptoms seemed to accompany these bouts with fear. When she reached the age of eleven, these bouts grew more numerous and lasted for longer periods of time. A thorough medical examination revealed no physical problem which could account for the colitis and nausea. Gradually the problem began to follow a pattern. Each night, as bedtime approached, the symptoms would appear. Terrifying fear would engulf her; her nausea was so pronounced that she would insist upon having a container by her bed in case she might vomit; the colitis symptoms would constantly plague her efforts to sleep. Her tears and fears combined to bring grave concern into our home. Medical science seemed to have no answer. The possibility of counseling was suggested for this possible psychosomatic illness.

It was about this time that the Lord was giving me some new insights into the importance of aggressive spiritual warfare. The Word of God was coming alive in my life concerning this important subject. I began to wonder if our daughter's problem could be caused by some demonic affliction. I shared my concern with my dear wife, and together we began to pray for divine wisdom as to whether this could be the problem.

I was reluctant even to mention the possibility to our daughter, lest her reaction might be greater fear and harm. I now see what a disservice this was to her. When the truth was finally shared with her, response was very positive and proved to be one of the great growing experiences of her life.

We began to realize the reality of demonic affliction through the power of prayer. On several occasions when our daughter was under greatest distress, I would go into her room and kneel by her bed. Taking her trembling, moist hands into mine, I would begin to pray silently over her in this manner:

"Loving heavenly Father, I bring my lovely daughter to your throne in prayer. Through the person and work of the Lord Jesus Christ, I present her to You as one made perfect and acceptable unto You. May the blessed Holy Spirit overshadow us during this time of prayer and enable me to pray in the Spirit. I bring all powers of darkness seeking to assault Judy and afflict her to account before the true and living God. I pray her union with the mighty victory of the Lord Jesus Christ directly against them. All powers of darkness seeking to hurt my daughter's body and soul, I bind up in the name of the Lord Jesus Christ. I loose her from their attack and plead over her the precious blood of the Lord Jesus Christ. As her father and as a priest of God, I claim my place of full authority over all powers of darkness. In Your grace, we receive this experience as one having purpose in the sovereign purposes of God. Teach Judy and our family through this trial. In the name of the Lord Jesus Christ. Amen."

During this kind of praying, on repeated occasions the symptoms would subside and disappear completely. She would be able to go to sleep and rest well, awakening refreshed and ready to face another day. I was now fairly certain that the problem was demonic, and I intensified my own prayer intercession much as outlined in the previous chapter. The results, though gratifying in these limited recessions, were not lasting. In fact, the severity of the attacks actually seemed to increase. I have since come to know that this is a good sign. One of two things usually happens when one enters into aggressive warfare in any particular problem. Both are good. Sometimes if the affliction is light, the results are immediately positive, and greater freedom results. At other times the attack may intensify for a time. This is the enemy's way of striking back and seeking to turn us aside from our resolve to enjoy our victory in Christ.

My hope was that I would be able to see my daughter set free by intercessory prayer alone. Because of her youth, I did not want to have to engage in any bold challenge of these powers of darkness who were intruding against my daughter. However, as I saw the increasing evidence of the enemy's resolve to hurt my daughter, I began to wonder if the Lord might not want me to face the enemy head-on, with my daughter's cooperation. She knew of my work helping others and had often prayed with our family for others who were afflicted. Carefully I began to share with Judy my concern that her fears and the physical manifestations might be demonic. I discovered to my joy that she had already considered this and was herself praying in warfare prayer against the enemy. I shared with her that our Lord might have a purpose in my boldly confronting these powers and commanding them to leave her presence forever. She hoped it might not be necessary, but agreed to pray with me about it.

The crisis arrived one night, as I was sharing a rare evening at home alone with Judy. The rest of the family was out, and the two of us had a good time just being together. When her bedtime arrived, she was once again under great stress. Fear overwhelmed her, nausea was particularly strong, her abdominal area was in great distress. We'd had enough. I asked her if she was ready to let me work directly against these afflicting powers. She, too, was fully prepared. Since the purpose of this book is to provide a handbook for guidance in spiritual warfare, I want to share as accurately as I can recall, the procedures and results that followed.

We went downstairs where we could have privacy and where we could be away from the phone and other possible distractions. I read several portions from God's Word which speak of our great victory and the power of our Lord over all of Satan's kingdom. Judy then prayed, committing her life and whole being into the hands of her Lord and Saviour. I then prayed a very extensive warfare prayer, much as has been already mentioned in the chapter on doctrine and aggressive prayer. While I was praying this time, Judy began to have intensive reactions. She described it as a dizzy sensation, as though the room were moving around. Everything she looked at began to be distorted in size and shape.

At this point I began to command for the powers of darkness afflicting her to come to manifestation. I called them before her faculties and commanded them to answer my questions. Following is an example of how this was done:

"In the name of the Lord Jesus Christ, I command Satan and all wicked spirits who do not have specific assignment against Judy to leave our presence. I resist you, sted-fast in the faith and on the authority of God's Word command you to leave our presence. We do not allow any interference or intrusion into our warfare against the powers of darkness afflicting Judy. I command all powers of darkness afflicting Judy to be bound aside. You may not work. You may not hurt her in any way. There is to be one-way traffic, out of Judy's life and to the place where the Lord Jesus Christ sends you. You may never return to afflict Judy. I call you before Judy's faculties. You must answer my questions by giving clear answers through her mind. You may not speak otherwise. I want no talk from you but answers to my questions. I command the chief power of darkness in charge of this affliction of fear, nausea, and all related problems to come to attention. I call you to account in the name of the Lord Jesus Christ. What is your name?"

During this time, Judy continued to face times of reeling sensations of nausea and distress. If they were severe, I would command the power to release her, and immediately there was relief. After some length of time, just continuing to command in the above-described manner, we were able to get the names of a hierarchy that was set on destroying Judy and through her problems would be able to attack my ministry. Some of the names given were identical to the symptoms described. Fear was the head of the hierarchy; under him were such workers as Nausea, Colon, Destroyer, and Deceiver.

Finally, after I was satisfied that the powers of darkness were fully exposed, I proceeded to command their departure in the following manner:

"In the name of the Lord Jesus Christ, I bind you all together. I bind all workers and helpers together. I bind to fear all hidden replacer or no-name demons that work under him. When Fear goes, all of his kingdom must go with him. You may not hurt Judy when you leave her presence. I command you to go where the Lord Jesus Christ sends you. I command you to go now. Go to the pit pre-

121

pared for you in the name of the Lord Jesus Christ."

After a period of working this way, there was a sweet release. The reeling symptoms disappeared, and Judy began to cry softly. I then asked the Holy Spirit to come and sweetly minister His fullness, His peace and joy to her life. We sang some hymns and choruses of joy and praise to our Lord. Great was the victory of our God. We had to work again on a couple of later occasions against other hierarchies, but the victory and deliverance was immediate. The fear, nausea, and other symptoms disappeared. This experience proved to be one of the most blessed in our lives. Judy has learned how to pray the truth of God in a wondrous manner against the enemy. I'd as soon have her prayers for me as anyone I know. Great has been the goodness of God through this experience to our entire family.

This is only one of many such bold encounters with the enemy of our souls that I have faced with those who have sought help. Judy agreed and wanted me to share her experience in this book, realizing that it well may help others who are under affliction and attack but do not know what to do. We have exposed this encounter as an example from our own warfare to illustrate and encourage other believers in their warfare.

I must raise some cautions and warnings lest some might be prone to rush into bold encounter carelessly. The counselor must not be presumptuous or trifling in these matters. Such bold warfare should always be accompanied by deep and total commitment to the Lordship of Jesus Christ. Such warfare requires careful doctrinal study on the ground of our victory. Scripture memorization should be the practice of your life, that the Sword of the Spirit will be ready to use. The snarling, wicked powers of darkness will do all they can to intimidate and frighten you in such encounters. Their tricks and deceptions are varied and numerous. Complete dependence upon the Holy Spirit and the victory of Christ alone will suffice to see one through to victory.

One should not work with any person in this bold confrontation unless that person is committed to surrender to the Lordship of Jesus Christ. The Lord seemed to give us such warnings in several places in the Bible. To the impotent man healed by our Lord in John 5 Jesus warns, "Behold, thou art made whole: sin no more, lest a worse thing come unto thee" (Jn 5:14).

Both Matthew and Luke record the warnings of our Lord in very sobering words: "When the unclean spirit is gone out of a man, he walketh through dry places, seeking rest; and finding none, he saith, I will return to my house whence I came out. And when he cometh, he findeth it swept and garnished. Then goeth he, and taketh to him seven other spirits more wicked than himself; and they enter in, and dwell there: and the last state of that man is worse than the first" (Lk 11:24-26; cf. Mt 12:43-45).

These verses remind us that we face an enemy who does not play games. He is a relentless, strategizing enemy. He never gives up. If a person only gets free from some demonic affliction and fails to fill up his life with the Word and the Holy Spirit's fullness, he well may face worse problems ahead than what he had before the bold confrontation.

Spiritual warfare is not a trifling matter. It requires the appropriation of all of our victory in the Lord Jesus Christ and a daily, close abiding in Christ. Sins of the flesh must not be tolerated and dismissed lightly. Worldliness does not belong in the believer's life. Those Christians who treat lightly these oft-repeated admonitions of the Word will find themselves easy pawns of Satan's sneaky ways. They may find it difficult to admit even to themselves that they are under Satan's bondage, but the enemy will be relentlessly at it. He uses every opportunity we give him to claim ground against the believer and to move in with his affliction and subtle bondage.

I would say humbly that no one ever becomes an expert in these times of confronting the enemy head-on. The moment he regards himself as such, he will be quickly humbled. Our only ground of victory over these powers is our union with the Lord Jesus Christ and the ministry of the Holy Spirit. Almost every time one faces a confrontation against darkness, he will find himself completely baffled as to what to do next. The powers of darkness are unpredictable and very crafty. Constant dependence upon the Holy Spirit for wisdom is necessary.

There are some dos and don'ts which should be emphasized in confrontation warfare.

Don't seek information or allow any wicked spirit to volunteer information you do not seek. Your communication with them has only the purpose of breaking their power and commanding them to leave. Other communication borders on what is condemned in Scripture as spiritism.

Don't believe what a wicked spirit says unless you test it. They are inveterate liars like their leader Satan. Command where information is received, "Will that answer stand as truth before the throne of the true and living God?"

Don't be afraid of their threatening of harm to you or your family. It is good to use 1 John 5:18b, "He that is begotten of God keepeth himself, and that wicked one toucheth him not" (KJV). They will often threaten to kill you or to destroy your loved ones. Our protection is the Lord, and they cannot hurt us when our Lord is shielding us.

Don't assume that one victory is the end of the warfare. Those afflicted with deep struggles with darkness find it necessary to maintain a close walk with the Lord Jesus. If one hierarchy has its power broken against you, another that has no direct relation to the former may manifest itself.

Don't rely upon bold confrontation as the main way to victory over the enemy. The positive application of doctrine, warfare praying, Scripture memorization, and a walk of praise toward God are very essential.

Do daily put on the whole armor of God and claim your union with Christ and walk in the fullness of the Holy Spirit.

Do take back all ground you may have given Satan by careless willful sins of the flesh. A simple prayer of faith accomplishes this. "In the name of the Lord Jesus Christ, I take back from Satan the ground I gave him when I lied to my boss. I confess this as sin against my Lord and ask for Your cleansing through the blood of Christ." This should also be a practice suggested to anyone you are called upon to help.

Do bind all powers of darkness working under any wicked spirit to him, commanding them all to leave when he does.

Do force the wicked spirit to admit that because you are seated with Christ far above all principalities and powers (Eph 1:21; 2:6) that you have full authority over them. They hate to admit this because it weakens their hold, but insist upon it on the ground of the Word.

Do force them to admit that when you command them to leave that they have to go where Christ sends them.

Do demand that if the wicked power has divided into several parts, that he become a whole spirit.

Do be prepared for the wicked power to try to hurt the person you are working with in some manner. Sudden body pains, a severe headache, a choking experience, and the like, are very often used. Command the power, naming the symptom, to release this hold immediately in the name of the Lord Jesus Christ.

As I close this chapter, may I caution that we must never assume all physical and emotional disorders to be demonic. Kurt Koch's book *Occult Bondage and Deliverance*, Part 2, provides a careful evaluation of how to determine what may be demonic and what may be purely physical or emotional problems that come from other causes.† It is important to know that our victory in Christ is full and complete over all of Satan's kingdom. Yet almost equally important is not to assign to Satan that which he is not causing. Giving credit to the enemy when he is not involved is a subtle way of giving him undeserved honor.

†Kurt Koch, *Occult Bondage and Deliverance* (Grand Rapids: Kregel, 1970).

10

CHALLENGING SATAN'S HINDRANCE OF REVIVAL

"Restore us, O God of our salvation, and cause Thine indignation toward us to cease. Wilt Thou be angry with us forever? Wilt Thou prolong Thine anger to all generations? Wilt Thou not Thyself revive us again, That Thy people may rejoice in Thee?" (Ps 85:4-6, NASB).

FOR MANY YEARS the Lord has burdened my heart for revival. I know that many other believers share this burden. We see with ever-increasing evidence that the only hope for our nation or world is revival. The mountainous wickedness of our time can only be stopped by God's severe judgment or by a mighty move of God's Spirit, authoring deep repentance and faith toward God.

We see many evidences of God's moving in our day. He is holding out to us the rich treasury of His grace. He is blessing and honoring various college campus movements with their great emphasis on personal evangelism and the Spirit-filled life. Great citywide and countrywide crusades are reaching many. Bible-preaching local churches with aggressive evangelism programs are also enjoying good growth amid the sea of wickedness which characterizes our times. Seminars which stress the overview of the biblical principles of living are enjoying phenomenal growth. Multiplied hundreds of thousands are taking such seminars on the Christian family, the marriage relationship, and other areas. The charismatic movement, despite its potentially dangerous overemphasis upon supernatural experience and emotion irrespective of doctrinal importance, has been used to introduce many to saving faith in the Lord Jesus Christ.

Yet despite all of these good tokens of God's grace, revival has not come. During the very time of the rapid growth of some of these movements, the moral decadence of society, the drug epidemic, crimes of violence and murder, and the general advances of sin and corruption go on unhampered. Multitudes of believers are worldly, apathetic, and indifferent to the cause of Christ. Revival has not come.

A few years ago, I was walking and praying in the church very early in the morning. I was experiencing unusual unction and enablement of the Holy Spirit as I pled for the Lord to pour out a revival upon our needy country and world. Suddenly the Lord moved upon my heart to know that before revival could come, there would have to be a very direct encounter with Satan. I was startled and confused for a moment, so much so that I stopped praying. I wondered what that meant.

In the busy life of the pastorate, I soon forgot that experience in prayer. Time passed, and I went through the traumatic time every pastor experiences when he is called to a new pastorate. Settled in my new responsibilities, the burden for revival continued to lie heavy on my heart.

On another occasion while walking and praying in the sanctuary early in the morning, the prayer for revival was unusually strong and deep. Once again there was that sudden awareness from the Lord that before there could be revival there would have to be a strong encounter with Satan. I was as startled and surprised as before. However, this time I went on in prayer. I said in essence, "All right, Lord, but I don't know what this means. I know very little

127

about Satan or his kingdom. I don't know anyone who does that I would consider sound in his doctrine. If You have someone ready to teach me what You want me to know, I'm ready to learn."

It was only a few days later that through a series of events, the Lord began to open up to me the subject of spiritual warfare. It is an ever-growing and learning experience for me.

I have come to see how very important spiritual warfare is to the subject of revival. It is important both to the bringing in of revival blessings and to the sustaining of the fruit of any great move of God. Satan hates the subject of revival more than any other burden of the church. Revivals have jarred and sent into retreat the kingdom of darkness as no other events ever have. Satan will do everything and anything he can to stop a revival. If it should come, he will immediately begin to corrupt and divert the movement from the Spirit of God's great work.

One sees this illustrated in the Word in the great move of God's Spirit at Pentecost. Through persecution and attempting internal corruption through Ananias and Sapphira, the enemy was at work to quench and destroy the Holy Spirit's move. One of Paul's purposes in writing to the Ephesians, so full of their first love fire for the Lord, was to teach them warfare and its place in continuous revival.

At the turn of the century, the mighty Welsh revival moved through Wales. What a joy it is to read of that holy move of God! It was characterized by deep, broken repentance over sin, swelling tides of praise to God that often went on for days and nights, and evangelism that saw whole villages and the larger part of cities converted. Yet almost immediately, Satan began to move against this great work of grace.

J. C. Metcalfe has written the foreword to the abridged edition of *War on the Saints*. In the foreword, Metcalfe makes this statement: "An aftermath of the Welsh Revival at the dawn of the present century was the rise of a number of extreme cults, often stressing a return to 'pentecostal'

128

practices. Mrs. Penn-Lewis, who had witnessed much of the Revival as the representative of *The Life of Faith*, saw clearly the peril of these fanatical teachings, and in collaboration with Mr. Evan Roberts, who played so prominent a part in the Revival, wrote a book, *War On The Saints*. In this book these extreme and overbalanced beliefs and practices are categorically branded as the work of an invading host of evil spirits. The word 'deception' might be said to be the key word in the book—a term which is in complete harmony with the findings both of John Wesley and Dr. Henson."*

This book, *War On The Saints*, is a classic in the study of Satan's war against believers. It is of interest to note that it was written after a revival had begun to wane and lose its thrust because of Satan's clever work. How necessary that we who desire revival should read such a book and study the Word that we might know how to battle Satan when revival comes.

Satan is the great imitator. When he comes as an angel of light, he is very difficult to spot. The Lord Jesus warned, "For there shall arise false Christs, and false prophets, and shall shew great signs and wonders; insomuch that, if it were possible, they shall deceive the very elect. Behold, I have told you before" (Mt 24:24-25, KJV). The tendency in revival or any spiritual movement is to accept all supernatural manifestations as being authored by God. Such a tendency, according to these warnings of our Lord, is very dangerous. This is why the Word of God calls upon believers to try (test) the spirits to measure and evaluate with care that which appears to be good. As stated earlier, the Holy Spirit will not be offended by this trying of the spirits. He is the One who told us to do it. This is one of the reasons why I am greatly concerned about some segments of the charismatic movement, with its broad emphasis upon the baptism of the Spirit and the experience of speaking in tongues. A spirit of caution is rarely heard by the

*War on the Saints, rev. ed., ed. Jessie Penn-Lewis (Ft. Washington, Pa., Christian Literature Crusade, 1964), p. vii.

proponents of charismatic gifts. Luke 11:11-13 and Matthew 7:9-11 are often used to prove that there is no danger of wicked powers deceiving when you are asking for the Holy Spirit and good gifts from God. What is forgotten is that this same Lord is the One who urged us to try the spirits and to believe not every spirit. If I seek some experience which does not have a sound biblical foundation, I am opening my life to some deceiving spirit to come as an angel of light.

It is my grave concern that one of the serious threats to genuine Holy Spirit-sent revival is the current spread of the charismatic movement with its emphasis upon experience and its lack of stand on objective, doctrinal truth. I say this, realizing that God in His sovereign grace and love is working through the movement to bring many to Christ. The apostle Paul recognized the reality of the Lord's sovereignty to work and move when Christ is preached, even when the balance is not right in the lives of the ones doing the preaching (see Phil 1:14-18). The Lord is using the charismatic movement with its emotional fire as a rebuke to the coldness and stiffness of some of us who are lukewarm in fervor though sound in doctrine.

Revival that is going to last must be characterized by deep study and loyalty to the absolute truth of the Word of God. All experience must be measured and understood in light of the truth of the Word. Error that is contrary to God's Word must be repudiated, renounced, and removed from one's life and practice, or Satan will soon move in advantage against him. I have many friends and loved ones who are ardent advocates of the charismatic movement and do not see the dangers I seek to bring into view. I do not mean this expressed caution to be a blanket condemnation of the movement or of them. I have had to deal with too many oppressed and afflicted people, however, who have opened their lives to demonic forces while seeking some supernatural experience not to sound the alarm.

Yet regardless of where we may stand in relation to this charismatic phenomena, all true believers see the great need of revival. As I see it, revival comes when the Holy Spirit moves with mighty power upon believers whose hearts have been made ready through repentance, prayer, and expectant waiting upon God. The Holy Spirit first touches the believer with His refining holy fire and His breath of power, filling the heart with overflowing worship, joy, and humility before the true and living God. The blessings of revival invariably overflow and spill out upon the world, resulting in great conviction of sin and repentance toward God on the part of the lost.

I understand revival to be that which is authored by God in His grace. It means that God draws near with His power and holiness until sin becomes exceedingly sinful and sinners become broken before God. Revival is the grace which came to us through the incarnation, the cross, the resurrection, and the coming of the Holy Spirit, all being poured out upon us in large measure and sudden visit. It means that whole areas of people and even entire nations begin to come under the mighty moving and conviction of God. God moves in with His supernatural intervention and stops man in his downward plunge.

Revival ought to be the great cry to God on the part of every believer for this hour. Some argue that we are too near the second coming of Christ to expect revival. The time of the apostasy is upon us, they say, and we can only expect things to get worse and worse while we feebly hold on and endure to the end. Such a view must be balanced by our Lord's promise to pour out His Spirit upon all flesh in the last days. The fruit of revival is always in God's will and plan during this age of grace. It is never the will of God for His church to be apathetic and powerless.

Even the Laodicean church in Revelation 3 is offered revival by our Lord. After rebuking them for their spiritual lukewarmness and for their state of not knowing that they were "wretched, and miserable, and poor, and blind, and naked," he offers them revival. In verses 18-20 we read, "I counsel thee to buy of me gold tried in the fire, that thou mayest be rich; and white raiment, that thou mayest be clothed, and that the shame of thy nakedness do not appear; and anoint thine eyes with eyesalve, that thou mayest see. As many as I love, I rebuke and chasten: be zealous, therefore, and repent. Behold, I stand at the door, and knock: if any man hear my voice, and open the door, I will come in to him, and will sup with him, and he with me" (KJV).

Warfare for revival involves aggressive use of all we have in Christ. It means that I seriously war against my flesh with the weapons outlined earlier. It means that I overcome the world through my union with Christ and the total employment of my faith. It means aggressive use of the weapons of our warfare against Satan and claiming our God-granted mightiness to the pulling down of strongholds. Once again, I would submit as a pattern for study and use, a type of warfare prayer for revival.

Heavenly Father, I praise Your name for the grace that has come to me through the Lord Jesus Christ. I rejoice in the victory which You have provided for me to live above sin and failure. I come before You in confession and to plead Your mercy over my own sins, the sins of other believers, and the sins of our nation. Our nation stands before You, deserving Your wrath and judgment. I confess the sins of lukewarmness, apathy, and worldliness on the part of believers. I acknowledge before You the wickedness of our society and its deserving of judgment. I stand in to confess the awful affront to You which is represented in the drug epidemic, the drunkenness, the moral rottenness in the entertainment field, the crime increases of our land, and the lack of moral character in national leadership. I ask forgiveness and mercy for the religious sins of liberalism and the too-often harsh, bitter criticism and contentious spirit of fundamentalism. I grieve with You over the awful rise of interest in the occult and the open worship of Satan by wicked, deceived people. May You judge not this nation with wrath and fury as upon Sodom, but judge it with a mighty outpouring of conviction of sin.

May sinners groan under the burden of their guilt until the people cry out as did those at Pentecost, "What shall we do?"

I praise Your holy name that there is sufficient measure of grace through the Person and work of the Lord Jesus Christ to answer this cry. I plead the blood of the cross and the power of the resurrection against the wretched sins and rebellion of the hearts of men against God. I wait for the Holy Spirit to lead and prepare and bring us all to revival.

I recognize that Satan and the kingdom of darkness over which he rules have plotted and strategized against revival with relentless effort. Satan has built carefully his kingdom to oppose all that is holy and good.

In the name of the Lord Jesus Christ, I smash and pull down all of the strongholds that Satan has erected to hinder revival. I pray the focus of the mighty victory of the cross and the resurrection of the Lord Jesus Christ directly against Satan's plans to hinder revival. I pull down his strongholds of religious loyalties that blind and bind so many. I pull down his strongholds of prayerlessness and carelessness with the Word of God. I claim back for the Lord Jesus Christ the ground Satan is claiming as a means of hindering revival, and I affirm that Satan's plans were fully defeated through the cross and the resurrection of Jesus Christ. I pull down all of Satan's plans to divert revival when it comes. I call for the Holy Spirit to grant wisdom and discernment to the leaders of revival chosen by You to lead. May this revival for which I pray be greater than any that has ever come before. May it serve to purify the church and prepare it for the coming of our Lord. May it bring multitudes into the fold all over the world.

Loving Lord Jesus Christ, You invited us to come and buy of You that which we need for revival. Give us the gold tried in the fires of testing brought by Your sovereign power. Give us the white raiment of Your purity as You live Your life in us. Grant us the eyesalve of the Holy Spirit's anointing to see spiritual truth, to retain it, and to apply it in practice. I open the door to Your Lordship, dear Saviour. I invite You to come in to me personally and into Your church with a fresh visit and to be the sovereign Lord You are, that we all might fellowship with you in the deepness of Your love. I ask this all and bring it before You with praise in the merit and worthiness of the Lord Jesus Christ. Amen.

Are you praying warfare prayers of this type for revival? May God move upon all of our hearts to do so.

11

TOOLS FOR WARFARE

"Blessed is the man who perseveres under trial, because when he has stood the test, he will receive the victor's crown, the life God has promised to those who love him" (Ja 1:12).

A NUMBER OF YEARS AGO, a friend of mine presented me with an unexpected gift which has proven to be one of the most helpful gifts I've ever received. This man brought me a large carpenter's tool box jammed full of wrenches, hammers, saws, screwdrivers, nails, screws, and many other things that go with such a box. One might wonder why a pastor would treasure such a gift. It is a gift that has never ceased to be a treasure to me because I like to do things with my hands. There is nothing more frustrating than wanting to do some project around the home and not having the necessary tools. In my heart I thank my friend for that gift every time I use it. The tools work for me in enabling me to get the job done.

We need tools in spiritual warfare as well. It has been the underlying purpose of this book to provide practical, usable information and insight into the waging of a winning warfare. The world, the flesh, and the devil will be continuously defeated if we use the weapons of our warfare.

The Lord has provided all the tools we need. The Lord Jesus Christ has provided all of our victory. He used the same tools He has provided us in winning the battle. His victory is our victory. It remains our responsibility to use these weapons so graciously provided in His grace. Every time you use them you'll thank God for the tools of victory He has provided. Just as I think with fond remembrance of the man who gave me the tool box when I use my carpenter's tools, so your heart will reach out in an ever-deepening gratitude to your Lord.

In previous chapters, importance of doctrinal truth and doctrinal praying was intended to be lifted high. Doctrine, God's unchanging truth, is mighty in defeating our enemies. This truth must get deep into our souls. This can only come about as we gain understanding of the Holy Word of God and then use that Word aggressively in our lives. With the permission and approval of Dr. Victor Matthews, professor of theology at the Grand Rapids Baptist Bible College and Seminary, I include here some very fine helps in keeping doctrinal truth in the forefront of your warfare.

"The Daily Affirmation of Faith" was written by Dr. Matthews to provide a concise, clear statement of the truth of the Word of God as it applies to our victory. I commend this affirmation for daily reading aloud on the part of those who are experiencing intense warfare. It will do much to build spiritual foundation into your soul. It will keep the ground of your victory aggressively in action against your enemies. Study the texts of Scripture for your own enlightenment and edification.*

THE DAILY AFFIRMATION OF FAITH

Today I deliberately choose to submit myself fully to God as He has made Himself known to me through the Holy Scripture which I honestly accept as the only inspired, infallible, authoritative standard for all life and

*Many helpful enlargements on the importance of these doctrines may be found in Victor Matthews, *Growth in Grace* (Grand Rapids: Zondervan, 1971).

practice. In this day I will not judge God, His work, myself, or others on the basis of feelings or circumstances.

1. I recognize by faith that the triune God is worthy of all honor, praise, and worship as the Creator, Sustainer, and End of all things. I confess that God, as my Creator, made me for Himself. In this day I therefore choose to live for Him (Rev 5:9-10; Is 43:1, 7, 21; Rev 4:11).

2. I recognize by faith that God loved me and chose me in Jesus Christ before time began (Eph 1:1-7).

3. I recognize by faith that God has proven His love to me in sending His Son to die in my place, in whom every provision has already been made for my past, present, and future needs through His representative work, and that I have been quickened, raised, seated with Jesus Christ in the heavenlies, and anointed with the Holy Spirit (Ro 5:6-11; 8:28-39; Phil 1:6; 4:6-7, 13, 19; Eph 1:3; 2:5-6; Ac 2:1-4, 33).

4. I recognize by faith that God has accepted me, since I have received Jesus Christ as my Lord and Saviour (Jn 1:12; Eph 1:6); that He has forgiven me (Eph 1:7); adopted me into His family, assuming every responsibility for me (Jn 17:11, 17; Eph 1:5; Phil 1:6); given me eternal life (Jn 3:36; 1 Jn 5:9-13); applied the perfect righteousness of Christ to me so that I am now justified (Ro 5:1; 8:3-4; 10:4); made me complete in Christ (Col 2:10); and offers *Himself* to me as my daily sufficiency through prayer and the decisions of faith (1 Co 1:30; Col 1:27; Gal 2:20; Jn 14:13-14; Mt 21:22; Ro 6:1-19; Heb 4:1-3, 11).

5. I recognize by faith that the Holy Spirit has baptized me into the Body of Christ (1 Co 12:13); sealed me (Eph 1:13-14); anointed me for life and service (Ac 1:8; Jn 7:37-39); seeks to lead me into a deeper walk with Jesus Christ (Jn 14:16-18; 15:26-27; 16:13-15; Ro 8:11-16); and to fill my life with Himself (Eph 5:18).

6. I recognize by faith that only God can deal with sin and only God can produce holiness of life. I confess that in my salvation my part was only to receive Him and that He dealt with my sin and saved me. Now I confess that in

order to live a holy life, I can only surrender to His will and receive Him as my sanctification; trusting Him to do whatever may be necessary in my life, without and within, so I may be enabled to live today in purity, freedom, rest and power for His glory (Jn 1:12; 1 Co 1:30; 2 Co 9:8; Gal 2:20; Heb 4:9; 1 Jn 5:4; Jude 24).

Having confessed that God is worthy of all praise, that the Scriptures are the only authoritative standard, that only God can deal with sin and produce holiness of life, I again recognize my total dependence upon Him and submission to Him. I accept the truth that praying in faith is absolutely necessary for the realization of the will and grace of God in my daily life (1 Jn 5:14-15; Ja 2:6; 4:2-3; 5:16-18; Phil 4:6-7; Heb 4:1-13; 11:6, 24-28).

Recognizing that faith is a total response to God by which the daily provisions the Lord has furnished in Himself are appropriated, *I therefore make the following decisions of faith:*

1. *For this day* (Heb 3:6, 13, 15; 4:7) I make the decision of faith to surrender wholly to the authority of God as He has revealed Himself in the Scripture — *to obey Him.* I confess my sin, face the sinful reality of my old nature, and deliberately choose to walk in the light, in step with Christ, throughout the hours of this day (Ro 6:16-20; Phil 2:12-13; 1 Jn 1:7, 9).

2. *For this day* I make the decision of faith to surrender wholly to the authority of God as revealed in the Scripture — *to believe Him.* I accept only His Word as final authority. I now believe that since I have confessed my sin He has forgiven and cleansed me (1 Jn 1:9). I accept at full value His Word of promise to be my sufficiency and rest, and will conduct myself accordingly (Ex 33:1; 1 Co 1:30; 2 Co 9:8; Phil 4:19).

3. *For this day* I make the decision of faith to recognize that God has made every provision so that I may fulfill His will and calling. Therefore, I will not make any excuse for my sin and failure (1 Th 5:24).

4. *For this day* I make the decision of faith deliberately

to receive from God that provision which He has made for me. I renounce all self-effort to live the Christian life and to perform God's service; renounce all sinful praying which asks God to change circumstances and people so that I may be more spiritual; renounce all drawing back from the work of the Holy Spirit within and the call of God without; and renounce all nonbiblical motives, goals, and activities which serve my sinful pride.

a. I now sincerely receive Jesus Christ as my sanctification, particularly as my cleansing from the old nature, and ask the Holy Spirit to apply to me the work of Christ accomplished for me in the crucifixion. In cooperation with and dependence upon Him, I obey the command to "put off the old man" (Ro 6:1-14; 1 Co 1:30; Gal 6:14; Eph 4:22).

b. I now sincerely receive Jesus Christ as my sanctification, particularly as my enablement moment by moment to live above sin, and ask the Holy Spirit to apply to me the work of the resurrection so that I may walk in newness of life. I confess that only God can deal with my sin and only God can produce holiness and the fruit of the Spirit in my life. In cooperation with and dependence upon Him, I obey the command to "put on the new man" (Ro 6:1-4; Eph 4:24).

c. I now sincerely receive Jesus Christ as my deliverance from Satan and take my position with Him in the heavenlies, asking the Holy Spirit to apply to me the work of the ascension. In His Name I submit myself to God and stand against all of Satan's influence and subtlety. In cooperation with and dependence upon God, I obey the command to "resist the devil" (Eph 1:20-23; 2:5; 4:27; 6:10-18; Col 1:13; Heb 2:14-15; Ja 4:7; 1 Pe 3:22; 5:8-9).

d. I now sincerely receive the Holy Spirit as my anointing for every aspect of life and service for today. I fully open my life to Him to fill me afresh in obedience to the command to "be filled with the Holy Spirit" (Eph 5:18; Jn 7:37-39; 14:16-17; 15:26-27; 16:7-15; Ac 1:8).

Having made this confession and these decisions of

faith, I now receive God's promised rest for this day (Heb 4:1-13). Therefore, I relax in the trust of faith, knowing that in the moment of temptation, trial, or need, the Lord Himself will be there as my strength and sufficiency (1 Co 10:13).

*   *   *

Another doctrinal tool that has proved of great benefit to me and to many others is the "Warfare Prayer" composed by Dr. Matthews. As a theologian, his unique and thorough way of including sound doctrine in this prayer is most helpful. I would urge anyone facing obvious spiritual warfare to use this prayer daily. It is good to read it aloud as a prayer unto the Lord. Eventually one will be able to incorporate the doctrinal truths expressed into his own prayer life without reading it.

The devil hates this prayer. Usually before working with anyone who has deep demonic affliction, I will request that we read this prayer in unison. Many times the oppressed one can read only with great difficulty. Sometimes sight problems, voice problems, or mind confusion become so intense that the afflicted person can continue only with great effort. It is the truth of God that Satan cannot resist, and he vigorously fights it being applied against him. Those serious about warfare should daily use a prayer of this type along with other prayer examples shared in this book.

WARFARE PRAYER

Heavenly Father, I bow in worship and praise before You. I cover myself with the blood of the Lord Jesus Christ as my protection during this time of prayer. I surrender myself completely and unreservedly in every area of my life to Yourself. I do take a stand against all the workings of Satan that would hinder me in this time of prayer, and I address myself only to the true and living God and refuse any involvement of Satan in my prayer.

Satan, I command you, in the name of the Lord

140

Jesus Christ, to leave my presence with all your demons, and I bring the blood of the Lord Jesus Christ between us.

Heavenly Father, I worship You, and I give You praise. I recognize that You are worthy to receive all glory and honor and praise. I renew my allegiance to You and pray that the blessed Holy Spirit would enable me in this time of prayer. I am thankful, heavenly Father, that You have loved me from past eternity, that You sent the Lord Jesus Christ into the world to die as my substitute that I would be redeemed. I am thankful that the Lord Jesus Christ came as my representative, and that through Him You have completely forgiven me; You have given me eternal life; You have given me the perfect righteousness of the Lord Jesus Christ so I am now justified. I am thankful that in Him You have made me complete, and that You have offered Yourself to me to be my daily help and strength.

Heavenly Father, come and open my eyes that I might see how great You are and how complete Your provision is for this new day. I do, in the name of the Lord Jesus Christ, take my place with Christ in the heavenlies with all principalities and powers (powers of darkness and wicked spirits) under my feet. I am thankful that the victory the Lord Jesus Christ won for me on the cross and in His resurrection has been given to me and that I am seated with the Lord Jesus Christ in the heavenlies; therefore, I declare that all principalities and powers and all wicked spirits are subject to me in the name of the Lord Jesus Christ.

I am thankful for the armor You have provided, and I put on the girdle of truth, the breastplate of righteousness, the sandals of peace, the helmet of salvation. I lift up the shield of faith against all the fiery darts of the enemy, and take in my hand the sword of the spirit, the Word of God, and use Your Word against all the forces of evil in my life; and I put on this armor and live and pray in complete dependence upon You, blessed Holy Spirit.

I am grateful, heavenly Father, that the Lord Jesus Christ spoiled all principalities and powers and made a show of

141

them openly and triumphed over them in Himself. I claim all that victory for my life today. I reject out of my life all the insinuations, the accusations, and the temptations of Satan. I affirm that the Word of God is true, and I choose to live today in the light of God's Word. I choose, heavenly Father, to live in obedience to You and in fellowship with Yourself. Open my eyes and show me the areas of my life that would not please You. Work in my life that there be no ground to give Satan a foothold against me. Show me any area of weakness. Show me any area of my life that I must deal with so that I would please You. I do in every way today stand for You and the ministry of the Holy Spirit in my life.

By faith and in dependence upon You, I put off the old man and stand into all the victory of the crucifixion where the Lord Jesus Christ provided cleansing from the old nature. I put on the new man and stand into all the victory of the resurrection and the provision He has made for me there to live above sin. Therefore, in this day, I put off the old nature with its selfishness, and I put on the new nature with its love. I put off the old nature with its fear and I put on the new nature with its courage. I put off the old nature with its weakness and I put on the new nature with its strength. I put off today the old nature with all its deceitful lusts and I put on the new nature with all its righteousness and purity.

I do in every way stand into the victory of the ascension and the glorification of the Son of God where all principalities and powers were made subject to Him, and I claim my place in Christ victorious with Him over all the enemies of my soul. Blessed Holy Spirit, I pray that You would fill me. Come into my life, break down every idol and cast out every foe.

I am thankful, heavenly Father, for the expression of Your will for my daily life as You have shown me in Your Word. I therefore claim all the will of God for today. I am thankful that You have blessed me with all spiritual blessings in heavenly places in Christ Jesus. I am thankful that

You have begotten me unto a living hope by the resurrection of Jesus Christ from the dead. I am thankful that You have made a provision so that today I can live filled with the Spirit of God with love and joy and self-control in my life. And I recognize that this is Your will for me, and I therefore reject and resist all the endeavors of Satan and of his demons to rob me of the will of God. I refuse in this day to believe my feelings, and I hold up the shield of faith against all the accusations and against all the insinuations that Satan would put in my mind. I claim the fullness of the will of God for today.

I do, in the name of the Lord Jesus Christ, completely surrender myself to You, heavenly Father, as a living sacrifice. I choose not to be conformed to this world. I choose to be transformed by the renewing of my mind, and I pray that You would show me Your will and enable me to walk in all the fullness of the will of God today.

I am thankful, heavenly Father, that the weapons of our warfare are not carnal, but mighty through God to the pulling down of strongholds, to the casting down of imaginations and every high thing that exalted itself against the knowledge of God, and to bring every thought into obedience to the Lord Jesus Christ. Therefore in my own life today I tear down the strongholds of Satan, and I smash the plans of Satan that have been formed against me. I tear down the strongholds of Satan against my mind, and I surrender my mind to You, blessed Holy Spirit. I affirm, heavenly Father, that You have not given us the spirit of fear, but of power and of love and of a sound mind. I break and smash the strongholds of Satan formed against my emotions today, and I give my emotions to You. I smash the strongholds of Satan formed against my will today, and I give my will to You, and choose to make the right decisions of faith. I smash the strongholds of Satan formed against my body today, and I give my body to You, recognizing that I am Your temple; and I rejoice in Your mercy and Your goodness.

Heavenly Father, I pray that now through this day You

would quicken me; show me the way that Satan is hindering and tempting and lying and counterfeiting and distorting the truth in my life. Enable me to be the kind of person that would please You. Enable me to be aggressive in prayer. Enable me to be aggressive mentally and to think Your thoughts after You, and to give You Your rightful place in my life.

Again, I now cover myself with the blood of the Lord Jesus Christ and pray that You, blessed Holy Spirit, would bring all the work of the crucifixion, all the work of the resurrection, all the work of the glorification, and all the work of Pentecost into my life today. I surrender myself to You. I refuse to be discouraged. You are the God of all hope. You have proven Your power by resurrecting Jesus Christ from the dead, and I claim in every way Your victory over all satanic forces active in my life, and I reject these forces; and I pray in the name of the Lord Jesus Christ with thanksgiving. Amen.

*   *   *

Some folks have questions about how they can determine if their problem is symptomatic of demonic affliction. Through experience and examples from the Word, I submit some symptoms which may indicate severe demonic affliction. These are not meant to be conclusive evidence of demonic affliction but are merely indicative of the enemy's work.

1. A compulsive desire to curse the Father, the Lord Jesus Christ, or the Holy Spirit.
2. A revulsion against the Bible, including a desire to tear it up or to destroy copies of the Word.
3. Compulsive suicidal or murderous thoughts.
4. Deep feelings of bitterness and hatred toward those for whom one has no reason to feel that way (e.g., the Jews, the church, strong Christian leaders).
5. Any compulsive temptation which seeks to force you to thoughts or behavior which you truly do not want to think or do.

144

6. Compulsive desires to tear other people down even if it means lying to do so. The vicious cutting use of the tongue may well be demonic. Satan will try to get you to attack anyone who is a threat to a problem area in your life.
7. Terrifying feelings of guilt and worthlessness even after honest confession of sin and failure is made to the Lord.
8. Certain physical symptoms which may appear suddenly or pass quickly for which there can be found no medical or physiological reason.
   a. Choking sensations.
   b. Pains which seem to move around and for which there is no medical cause.
   c. Feelings of tightness about the head or eyes.
   d. Dizziness, blackouts, or fainting seizures.
9. Deep depression and despondency.
10. Terrifying seizures of panic and other abnormal fears.
11. Dreams and nightmares that are of a horrific, recurring nature. Clairvoyant dreams—dreams that later come true—may well be demonic. One can usually eliminate this problem by remembering to say a prayer like this before he goes to sleep each night: "In the name of the Lord Jesus Christ, I submit my mind and my dream activities only to the work of the Holy Spirit. I bind up all powers of darkness and forbid them to work in my dream abilities or any part of my subconscious while I sleep."
12. Sudden surges of violent rage, uncontrollable anger, or seething feelings of hostility.
13. Terrifying doubt of one's salvation even though one once knew the joy of this salvation.

From the example of the deeply troubled man of Gadara we glean some clues to the wicked workings of deep demonic affliction. In his personal, unpublished notes, Ernest Rockstad calls attention to six symptoms of the man's demonic torment:

a. Incapacity for normal living. He couldn't live in society. He had a greater kinship with death than with life.
b. Violence and superhuman strength. Chains and fetters could not hold him.
c. Grave personality and behavior problems. "Neither could any man tame him." The person who can be sweet and kind one minute and bitter and hateful the next may indicate another control of the life.
d. Restlessness and insomnia. Luke 8:29 tells us this man was driven by demons. He couldn't sleep in the night. Demonically-caused insomnia can usually be remedied by the memorization and meditation on the Word of God while waiting to go to sleep.
e. A terrible inner anguish. This man went about "crying." So terrible were the inner pressures and torments that he had to cry out.
f. Self-inflicted injury. He cut himself with stones. One reason for this may have been that the physical pain helped relieve the inner anguish and torment.

The problem of transference is one which needs practical attention. This has been mentioned earlier, but I would like to amplify upon this important subject and suggest steps for defeating this problem. By transference we mean the passing on of demonic powers from one generation to the next. Some of us are troubled as to how wicked powers of Satan can afflict little children. Examples of this problem can be cited in Scripture (e.g., Mk 9:14-29), from experience on the mission field, and from the experience of anyone who has worked long in this realm of demonic affliction. Little children can be tormented and afflicted by some demonic power. On what ground or by what avenue can the powers of darkness trouble an innocent little one? It is not my purpose to explore the deep theological considerations of this problem, but rather to suggest some steps to defeat this obvious affliction.

The Old Testament Scriptures do give hint to the transferring of the sin problem from generation to generation. The inherited old nature itself is a transferred problem all the way from Adam. As God gave man the law, we have His sobering words, "For I the LORD thy God am a jealous God, visiting the iniquity of the fathers upon the children unto the third and fourth generation of them that hate me" (Ex 20:5 KJV; cf. Ex 34:7; Deut 5:9). The law of God that we reap what we sow extends on to our children and our children's children.

On one occasion I battled against a wicked spirit afflicting a very fine Christian young lady. This powerful enemy of darkness was particularly obstinate and tried to refuse to depart to where the Lord Jesus would send him. In the process of breaking down his resistance, I commanded him to reveal how long he had been in the family. He claimed to have first entered the family ancestral line on the ground of the girl's great grandmother's sin committed as a young woman in Glasgow, Scotland. Such incidents are not unusual. One wicked spirit claimed to have been working in the ancestral line for over five hundred years. We cannot build our procedures on the basis of demonic assertions, yet careful warfare demands that we not overlook this transfer problem.

Recently someone called my attention to the case of some dear Christian parents who have a son in prison. This son has been involved in the deepest kinds of brutal sin. He has been accused of rape, has been convicted as a drug pusher, and is bitter against all authority. He hates the church, God, and everything his Christian parents hold dear. They have trained him in the best surroundings and in a Bible-preaching church. He has led a terribly sick life from the time he was a young child. Further, he was an adopted child, and his problem behavior goes back to his very youngest days. Good environment had no power to change it. This kind of problem has been noted in other adoptive situations in a number of disturbing studies that have been made recently. As a pastor, I have observed this in several different painful family situations. One seriously wonders if it could be this problem of transference through generation blood lines of demonic affliction and possession.

Thank God that not all adoptive situations manifest such problems. But what can be done if such problems arise? If I recognize this problem, what can I as a Christian do about it? Let me suggest some warfare steps which can be taken.

For your own life and family, the following prayer and affirmation should be made. This renunciation and affirmation has been composed by the Reverend Ernest B. Rockstad of Faith and Life Ministries in Andover, Kansas. Ernest Rockstad is one of God's most experienced veterans in this subject of warfare.†

Renunciation and Affirmation

As a child of God purchased by the blood of the Lord Jesus Christ, I here and now renounce and repudiate all the sins of my ancestors. As one who has been delivered from the power of darkness and translated into the kingdom of God's dear Son, I cancel out all demonic working that has been passed on to me from my ancestors. As one who has been crucified with Jesus Christ and raised to walk in newness of life, I cancel every curse that may have been put upon me. I announce to Satan and all his forces that Christ became a curse for me when He hung on the cross. As one who has been crucified and raised with Christ and now sits with Him in heavenly places, I renounce any and every way in which Satan may claim ownership of me. I declare myself to be eternally and completely signed over and committed to the Lord Jesus Christ. All this I do in the name and authority of the Lord Jesus Christ (Ro 6:4; Gal 2:20; 3:13; Eph 1:7; 2:5-6; Co 1:13).

_____

(Name and Date)

Much helpful material on warfare may be secured by writing to Ernest B. Rockstad, 632 N. Prosperity Lane, Andover, Kansas 67002.

148

NOTE:
None of us knows what works of Satan may have been passed on to him from his ancestry. Therefore, it is well for every child of God to make the above renunciation and affirmation. It is advisable to speak it out loud.

*　　*　　*

Since the suggestion of the possibility of a transfer problem in adoptive situations has been made, let me suggest a renunciation and affirmation parents might employ for their adopted or foster children.

In the name of the Lord Jesus Christ, I praise my heavenly Father that He has entrusted to me my adopted child, _____. I accept all responsibility that God places upon me to be a parent and a priest of God in _____'s life. As a priest of God in my child's life, and purchased by the blood of the Lord Jesus Christ, I here and now renounce and repudiate all the sins of _____'s blood ancestors. In the name of the Lord Jesus Christ, I cancel out all demonic working that would want to be passed on to _____ from his blood ancestors. I aggressively announce against Satan and all of his forces that I cover _____ with the protection of the blood of the Lord Jesus Christ and the work of the Holy Spirit. As one who has authority over all powers of darkness through my union with the Lord Jesus Christ, and since I am seated with Him in heavenly places, I renounce any and every way in which Satan may claim ownership of _____. I pull down all blindness which Satan would put on _____'s eyes to keep him from understanding spiritual truth and growing to love and serve my Lord and Saviour. As the legal parent in the eyes of God and as a priest of God in _____'s life, I completely sign him over to the keeping and saving power of the Lord Jesus Christ. As a priest of God in _____'s life, I cancel and take back all ground given to Satan by his ancestors. I claim that ground through the victory over Satan achieved by the Lord Jesus Christ in His redemptive work and cover all ground with

His precious blood that Satan may have no claim against
_____. All of this I do in the name and authority of the
Lord Jesus Christ and will accept in my child's life only that
which comes by way of the cross and through God's grace.

(NAME AND DATE)

A renunciation and affirmation of this type should often
be a part of one's prayer ministry for his adopted child. As
the child comes to maturity, the careful, spiritually
minded parent should lead that child into his own use of
the weapons of his warfare.

Another important matter in warfare is the taking back
of ground we may give through our own fleshly or worldly
sins. Ephesians 4:27 warns, "Neither give place to the
devil." As has been mentioned earlier, it is possible for a
believer through fleshly sins or careless worldliness to
give place to the devil. If I know I have done this, how do I
reclaim all the ground for the Lord Jesus Christ? I would
suggest to start, having a quiet, shut-away time with the
Lord. Take a sheet of paper and begin to list the sins you
can recall from your life in which you know you gave
ground to the enemy. Ask the Holy Spirit to help you
remember all sins which have given Satan place against
you. Some areas of particular concern should be the following:
1. Any lying, deceiving acts on your part
2. Any time of giving way to sensual appetites or indulging in sexual sins
3. Any occasions of showing interest or involvement in
   occult practices or games
4. Any sin of questioning God's love and goodness toward
   you or others
5. Times of cursing or using your tongue viciously against
   others
6. Times when one might have misused God's Word or
   disbelieved its truth

7. Sins of stealing or coveting
8. Sins of indulging in violent outbursts of rage or anger.
This list need be seen by only your eyes. If you have sinned against another, it is necessary to ask forgiveness of that person to clear the offense and your conscience.

After you have made your list, it is good to go over the list in prayer by aggressively taking back the ground given. Here is a suggested prayer:

Blessed heavenly Father, I ask Your forgiveness for offending You by committing this sin of [name the offense]. I claim the cleansing that is mine through the blood of the Lord Jesus Christ. I address myself against Satan and all of his kingdom. I take away from you and all your powers of darkness any ground you are claiming against me when I sinned in [name the offense]. I claim that ground back in the name of the Lord Jesus Christ. I cover it with the blood of the Lord Jesus Christ and give all areas of my life over to the full control of the Holy Spirit.

It is good to keep one's heart constantly open to the Holy Spirit, asking Him to bring to mind any offense that gave the enemy a foothold against you. No matter what you are doing or where you are, should the Holy Spirit bring something to mind, you can immediately claim back all ground in a prayer of the type just mentioned.

A few words need to be shared with those who are under special attack of the enemy. Oppressive bondage from Satan is a very painful experience for believers. Some of the greatest suffering I have ever witnessed has been that caused by deep demonic affliction. Such warfare requires total commitment to the Lord and to aggressive warfare designed to set one free. Here is a checklist for daily usage by those so oppressed:

1. Daily resolve to believe God and to fight for your deliverance. Passivity and hopelessness is deadly defeat. They are the opposite of the three great virtues of Christianity: faith, hope, and love.
2. Daily thank God for your warfare and for what He is teaching you through the battle.

3. Break and pull down all relationships established by Satan and wicked spirits between yourself and others. Just as God authors relationships within His will and purpose, so our enemy seeks to author relationships between yourself and others. This can be broken by using a prayer of this type:

In the name of the Lord Jesus Christ I will accept only relationships between _____ and me that are authored by the Holy Spirit. I smash and break down all relationships between _____ and me that are authored by Satan or wicked Spirits.

If you sense that there might be demonic activity in another person's life, with whom you are experiencing tension, exercise a prayer of this type:

In the name of the Lord Jesus Christ I break and smash all strength and communication which the powers of darkness with assignment against me are trying to establish with _____ I smash and pull down all such communication and strength in the name of the Lord Jesus Christ.

4. Go through strong doctrinal praying every day, perhaps using one of the warfare prayers outlined earlier.
5. Reject aggressively all thoughts of discouragement, hopelessness, fear, and self-condemnation. These are out of harmony with one's position in Christ.
6. Keep your mind full of positive thoughts and declarations of faith. Words of hymns are a wonderful source for such positive thinking.
7. Affirm God's greatness, His love and goodness by faith. Never let satanically-caused feelings project into your mind doubt about God's greatness.
8. Memorize and meditate daily on the Word of God.
9. Seek to search out your true feelings and thoughts from those that are demonically caused. Reject all wrong thoughts in a prayer of this type:

In the name of the Lord Jesus Christ, I reject this thought and feeling of _____ which is contrary to

God's will. I choose to accept only thoughts in harmony with the Holy Spirit, and I cover my thought life with the blood of the Lord Jesus Christ.

10. If you fail and the enemy wins a battle, confess your failure to the Lord immediately, and keep with the fight. You may lose a few skirmishes, but you've already won the battle because you are united to Christ in His victory (Luke 10:17-20).

12

WARFARE THROUGH OUR ONENESS TOGETHER

"Live in harmony with one another. Don't be proud, but be willing to associate with people of low position. Don't be conceited" (Ro 12:16).

I HAVE BEEN WORKING on the final draft of this book while sitting by the fireplace. I've diligently tried to keep the fire going by using a combination of fireplace coal and some kindling wood. One of the problems I've faced is that the kindling wood tends to burn too rapidly. I've discovered something, however, that has an application to this matter of spiritual warfare. By taking some wire and binding the kindling into a close, tight bundle, I've discovered that it burns much more slowly, almost like a large log would burn. The devouring fire is much more limited as the kindling remains bound tightly together.

Something needs to be said about the vital importance of the unity, the closeness of the body of Christ in this matter of warfare. It has been stressed over and over in these pages that the believer's victory is his union to the Lord Jesus Christ who has won our victory. It is also important to see that in being united to Christ we are also united to all other members of Christ's body. "The body is a unit, though it is made up of many parts; and though all its parts are many, they form one body. So it is with Christ. For we are all baptized by one Spirit into one body—whether Jews or Greeks, slave or free—and we were all given the one Spirit to drink" (1 Co 12:12-13). "So in Christ we who are many form one body, and each member belongs to all the others" (Romans 12:5).

These verses say something very important to us, and they represent larger portions of the Word that remind us that believers must function as a unit, a body in close harmony and dependence upon one another. As believers remain tightly bound together and tightly bound to their Head, the devouring fires of Satan can do us little harm. One little piece of kindling trying to go it alone will surely be soon scorched.

Many times as I have worked to help folk get free from devastating demonic assault, I have longed for the vital involvement of large numbers of believers who would join in the fight through their intercessory prayers and encouragement. It is not unusual, however, for the troubled person to desperately want to keep his problem a secret from his Christian friends. He fears that they will think him some kind of a mental case who is to be avoided and talked about in gatherings where he is not present. Too often I've had to admit to myself that he is probably right. I know many dedicated Christians who would think any kind of serious and aggressive warfare with the devil and his kingdom to be an extremism to be avoided. Somehow, in God's grace and love and through the faithful teaching of God's Word, this situation must change. Believers must begin to see their deep and vital need of one another again. We must practice the truth that we are in this warfare together. "But God has combined the members of the body and has given greater honor to the parts that lacked it, so that there should be no division in the body, but that its parts should have equal concern for each other. If one part suffers, every part suffers with it; if one part is honored, every part rejoices with it" (1 Co 12:24-26).

It is fascinating to note that the great passages on spiritual warfare were not written just to individuals but to churches, organized bodies of believers. Perhaps the greatest passage in the Bible on spiritual warfare, Ephesians 6:10-18, closes with the reminder, "With this in mind, be alert and always keep on praying for *all* the saints" (6:18b, italics added). The apostle goes on to plead for their continued prayers for him, as he has repeatedly reminded them of his prayers for them.

From experience as well as from teaching the Word of God, I've seen how true the strength of a united body of believers is. There have been times when little progress is made in trying to help some soul get free from some afflicting demonic power. Appeal for prayer from several earnest believers who know the realities of such warfare makes the next session another story completely. The enemy is soon dispatched to where the Lord Jesus Christ sends him.

It is my deep concern that a book of this type not in any way divide the body of believers. Some will grasp hold of the concepts shared in this volume with eager zeal. Others may feel that the emphasis has been over-stressed. May I caution both positions not to be hasty in judging or criticizing each other. We must remember that we are members of the body of Christ, and we need each other. Prayer, study, and trusting the Holy Spirit will keep us moving forward, tightly bound together. "Make every effort to keep the unity of the Spirit through the bond of peace" (Eph 4:3).

We must never view ourselves as experts in this matter of spiritual warfare. The moment we do, we become the victims of our enemy. Only total humble reliance upon the Lord Jesus Christ can secure our victory. Never let this subject of warfare with Satan and his kingdom divide you from your union with the body of believers.

As believers, we are coming near the end. The coming of our Lord seems very near. The Middle East remains tense, Russia seems poised and could make a move against Israel one day not too far away. The sovereign plan of God is moving toward conclusion. Few prophetic scholars have any doubt of this.

This means that united believers are going to have to become more proficient in their usage of their weapons of warfare. The battle lines are being more aggressively drawn by the enemy of our souls. He is boldly intruding more openly into the affairs of men. He plans to fasten his grip tighter and tighter upon the world. He is moving his world system toward his ideal man's takeover when the Antichrist will rule. Christians united together and to Christ are his only real threat in the world system. He will do his best to divide and defeat us. He will seek to make the world appeal more strongly to our flesh than it ever has. He will send his demons against us more strongly than anything we have ever faced (1 Ti 4:1). We must be ready for the battle. This is the reason I have sought to share some of the things the Lord has shown me about our warfare. The day of halfway measures in spiritual warfare is past. Only as the united body steps into its purchased victory with aggressive application are we going to stand. Those who draw apart from the body and the Lord Jesus Christ will suffer painful spiritual defeat. They will enter into salvation and the joys of heaven through God's grace and keeping power, but will miss the strong joy of winning the battle. I humbly urge every reader of these words to fight a good fight and to love the body of Christ as our Lord loves it.

As the signs of our Lord's coming multiply and the intensity of the warfare increases, another fact is coming near also. The fact is that our warfare is nearing its end. The Lord Jesus Christ is coming soon to rule with a rod of iron. For the redeemed, this will signal the end of our warfare with the flesh. When He comes, the battle of a believer with his flesh shall suddenly and swiftly end, for "We shall not all sleep, but we shall all be changed, in a moment, in the twinkling of an eye, at the last trump: for the trumpet shall sound, and the dead shall be raised incorruptible, and we shall be changed" (1 Co 15:51-52, KJV). "Then we which are alive and remain shall be caught up together with them in the clouds, to meet the Lord in the air: and so shall we ever be with the Lord" (1 Th 4:17, KJV). Though we'll have bodies, they will be glorified ones, and that old nature we all know so well will be vanished away in the floods of our glorified righteous state. Our enemy, the flesh, will be no more.

The coming of the Lord Jesus Christ also ends the warfare with the world as we know it. Our Lord's rule in earth will be a rule of righteousness and peace. Satan's rule will end. The world order will be under the absolute sovereign rule of a righteous King. Those who rule with Him are the whole body of glorified saints. The world system will be judged at our Lord's coming, and its power as an extension of man's flesh and Satan's deception shall be eternally ended (Mt 25:31-34).

Our battle with the devil will also be ended at our Lord's return. Satan will be bound in the bottomless pit with all of his forces for a thousand years (Rev 20:1-6). Satan will not in any way be allowed to intrude his ugly work into the rule of our Lord.

As members of the body of Christ today, we are to close out what those early members of the body of Christ faced with intensity of warfare. Our battle promises to be just as fierce a combat as theirs. We need the same unity and oneness, the same confidence of victory, the same bold usage of our weapons, the same fearless assurance of our ground, and the same awareness that it is soon going to be over and we'll be home, enjoying our prize. We are "looking for that blessed hope, and the glorious appearing of the great God and our Saviour Jesus Christ" (Titus 2:13, KJV). "He which testifieth these things saith, Surely I come quickly. Amen. Even so, come, Lord Jesus" (Rev 22:20, KJV).

BIBLIOGRAPHY

Basham, Don. *Deliver Us from Evil*. Washington Depot, Conn.: Chosen, n.d.

Boshold, Frank S. *Blumhardt's Battle, a Conflict with Satan*. New York: Lowe, 1970.

Bounds, Edward M. *Satan: His Personality, Power, and Overthrow*. New York: F. H. Revell Co., 1922.

Breese, Dave. *His Infernal Majesty*. Chicago: Moody, 1974.

Briscoe, D. Stuart. *The Fullness of Christ*. Grand Rapids: Zondervan, 1971.

Chafer, Lewis Sperry. *Satan – His Motive and Methods*. Grand Rapids: Zondervan, 1969.

Demon Experiences in Many Lands. Chicago: Moody, 1960.

Dickason, C. Fred. *Angels, Elect and Evil*. Chicago: Moody, 1975.

Ernest, Victor H. *I Talked with Spirits*. Wheaton, Ill.: Tyndale, 1972.

Freeman, Hobart E. *Angels of Light?* Plainfield, N. J.: Logos, 1971.

Harper, Michael. *Spiritual Warfare*. Plainfield, N. J.: Logos, 1970.

Knight, Walker L. *The Weird World of the Occult*. Wheaton, Ill. Tyndale, 1972.

Koch, Kurt. *Between Christ and Satan*. Grand Rapids: Kregel, 1962.

———. *Occult Bondage and Deliverance*. Grand Rapids: Kregel, 1970.

———. *The Devil's Alphabet*. Grand Rapids: Kregel, 1969.

Lindsey, Hal. *Satan Is Alive and Well on Planet Earth*. Grand Rapids: Zondervan, 1972.

Lloyd-Jones, D. Martyn. *Authority*. Downers Grove, Ill.: Inter-Varsity Press, 1958.

159

MacMillan; J. A. *The Authority of the Believer*. Harrisburg, Pa.: Christian Pubns., n.d.

Manuel, Frances D. *Though an Host Should Encamp*. Ft. Washington, Pa.: Christian Literature Crusade, 1971.

McElheran, Clifton K. *Let the Oppressed Go Free*. North Platte, Neb.: Outreach for Christ, 1970.

Mercada, Dick. *Don't Dare Today's Demons!* Boston: Stuart, 1964.

Mounce, Robert. "Do Demons Possess People Today?" *Eternity*, February, 1973.

Nevius, John L. *Demon Possession and Allied Themes*. New York: Revell, 1893.

————. *Demon Possession*. Grand Rapids: Kregel, 1968.

Nee, Watchman. *The Spiritual Man*. 3 vols. New York: Christian Fellowship, 1968.

Orr, J. Edwin. *Campus Aflame*. Glendale, Cal.: Gospel Light, 1971.

————. *Are Demons for Real?* Wheaton, Ill. Scripture Press, 1970.

Pedigo, Jess. *Satanism—Diabolical Religion of Darkness*. Tulsa, Okla.: Christian Crusade, 1971.

Penn-Lewis, Jessie. *War on the Saints* (abridged edition). Ft. Washington, Pa.: Christian Literature Crusade, n.d.

Peterson, Robert. *Are Demons for Real?* Chicago: Moody, 1968.

Phillips, McCandlish. *The Spirit World*. Wheaton, Ill.: Victor, 1970.

Rockstad, E. B. Booklets and Pamphlets on Spiritual Warfare. Andover, Kan.: Rockstad, 67002.

Sanders, J. Oswald. *Satan Is No Myth*. Chicago: Moody, 1975.

Unger, Merrill F. *Demons in the World Today*. Wheaton, Ill.: Tyndale, 1971.

————. *Biblical Demonology*. Wheaton, Ill.: Scripture Press, 1965.

Usher, Charles H. *Satan a Defeated Foe*. Ft. Washington, Pa.: Christian Literature Crusade, n.d.

Whyte, H. A. Maxwell. *Hidden Spirits*. Scarborough, Ont.: Whyte, 1950.

Wiersbe, Warren W. *Be Real*. Wheaton, Ill.: Victor, 1972.

Wilburn, Gary A. *The Fortune Seller*. Glendale, Calif.: Regal, 1972.

Wright, J. Stafford. *Christianity and the Occult*. Chicago: Moody, 1972.